"Teens and young adults who are looking for practical, constructive tips to help them navigate life will enjoy Cheryl Bradshaw's *How to Like Yourself*. It's fun, easy to read, and upbeat—almost like having an extended conversation with your own mental health coach. The author's unique combination of professional training and experiences working with emerging adults, together with her energy and love of life, shine through on every page."

> —**Eric Windeler**, father, full-time advocate for youth mental health, and founder and executive director of www.jack.org

"Cheryl Bradshaw has written an engaging, powerful, and easy-to-read book in *How to Like Yourself*. To help teens combat their inner critic, she provides a step-by-step plan using proven-effective cognitive strategies. Her honest and genuine approach normalizes struggles with confidence and self-esteem, and makes it easy to work through the material. It's as though she is in the room with you!"

> —**Sheri Turrell, PhD**, registered psychologist in Toronto, ON, Canada, with over twenty years of experience in mental health, and coauthor of *ACT for Adolescents*

"Cheryl Bradshaw's words are exactly what my younger self needed to hear. As a teenager, I was really struggling. What was going on in my mind was the total opposite of liking myself. It wasn't until after high school that I even realized the power of my inner voice to change my own mind. It's awesome to think of other young people like me picking up this book and stumbling across this treasured secret: that what you tell yourself inside your head—no matter what's going on around you—makes all the difference in the world for your happiness and well-being."

> —**Erin Hodgson**, youth mental health advocate, motivational speaker, mental illness survivor, and champion of hope and recovery

"An important reminder from an honest and compassionate voice! Sometimes, when I'm not feeling great, I just feel like curling up on a comfy couch, under a blanket, with sunbeams coming through the windows. If you feel the same way sometimes, this book can help. Great job, Cheryl!"

—**Neil Pasricha**, *New York Times* best-selling author
of *The Happiness Equation* and *The Book of Awesome*

"Cheryl Bradshaw has given a voice to many thoughts, concerns, and insecurities most of us feel on a regular basis. In common language and with understanding, she helps her reader to consider different perspectives and strategies to counter negativity and patterns. She skillfully infuses humor to not only laugh at herself, but also to help us appreciate a lighter side of ourselves. This book is a must for preteens and millennium-aged adults who are considering self-reflection, improvement, or seeking insight into others."

—**Carol Nagy, MSW**, executive director of Niagara Hospice
in Lockport, NY, and, most importantly, mom to two
millennium-aged adults

"This is a lively, quick read with crucial information every teen needs. Self-love is an incredible anchor through the teen years and beyond. Cheryl Bradshaw addresses the topic thoroughly with tips and ideas to help teen readers get connected in a loving way to themselves!"

—**Lucie Hemmen, PhD**, clinical psychologist and author
of *The Teen Girl's Survival Guide*

"*How to Like Yourself* is refreshing, relatable, engaging, and essential. Super charming from start to finish."

—**Jesse Hayman**, director of community at the Movember
Foundation in Canada, founder and director of the nonprofit
I've Got A Story, and director of Gainline Africa

"*How to Like Yourself* is the book I wish I could have read in high school or after a bad breakup, but it's just as valuable now as a young adult trying to figure life out. Just liking who you are is an underrated yet powerful skill. Cheryl Bradshaw's writing is real. It's relatable. And it's practical stuff—without a lot of the cheese."

> —**Kayley Reed**, fashion designer, social entrepreneur, and cofounder and CEO of Wear Your Label, a clothing line designed to raise awareness about mental health

"Cheryl Bradshaw's book speaks directly to young people in a way that's engaging and understands where we are. It treats the reader like an equal, which is a refreshing and much-needed change from other books of this genre. I would recommend this book for all young folks who are having a hard time loving themselves."

> —**Alicia Raimundo**, international public speaker, and advocate for youth mental health activism and awareness

"When you know how to be a best friend to yourself, you will be happier, more confident, and you'll also make more friends! This book is a great start to the journey of liking and loving yourself!"

> —**Christine Arylo**, author of *Madly in Love with ME*, and founder of Self-Love Day

"*How to Like Yourself* teaches teens to do just that: like themselves. Developing this skill isn't easy as an adult, let alone a teen. Cheryl Bradshaw does an incredible job of uncovering the complexities involved in developing a positive relationship with oneself in a subtle, nonthreatening manner. I highly recommend this book and look forward to using it with the teens I work with!"

> —**Julia V. Taylor, MA**, author of *The Body Image Workbook for Teens*

"Bradshaw's voice reads like the wise companion I wish I'd had when battling insecurities and figuring out how to be okay with myself in early adulthood and beyond. Her use of urban language is refreshing, down-to-earth, and funny! This book is a comprehensive guide to navigating the relationship with self. It incorporates time-tested techniques from a psychotherapist's toolbox with real-life scenarios, and a sassy use of animated characters and images. After reading this book, you are bound to have a more insightful and compassionate relationship with yourself—a superb companion to have on this journey!"

—**Kanchan Kurichh, MA, RP**, psychotherapist and
college counselor

"In *How to Like Yourself*, Cheryl Bradshaw offers a smart and straightforward approach for teens and young adults to build a more positive and accepting mindset in their everyday lives. We've all struggled with being our own worst critic, and Bradshaw delivers easy-to-learn tools that translate in the real world with the perfect amount of humor and heart. In a relatable tone and with language that is easy to understand, Bradshaw takes the reader through an uplifting approach that will appeal to young readers. I highly recommend this to both parents looking for material to help their children build healthy self-esteem, and to teens looking to understand and love their true selves more."

—**Cadence Grace**, musician and member of the country
music trio Runaway Angel

"*How to Like Yourself* is a unique and charmingly written book that provides real, practical building blocks for developing self-esteem and confidence in those about to launch into the adult world. Approachable and honest, this book is a must for those who wish to live an enlightened and self-directed life."

—**Jennifer Silk, MACP**, mental health counselor, crisis worker,
and mom

the *i*nstant help solutions series

Young people today need mental health resources more than ever. That's why New Harbinger created the **Instant Help Solutions Series** especially for teens. Written by leading psychologists, physicians, and professionals, these evidence-based self-help books offer practical tips and strategies for dealing with a variety of mental health issues and life challenges teens face, such as depression, anxiety, bullying, eating disorders, trauma, and self-esteem problems.

Studies have shown that young people who learn healthy coping skills early on are better able to navigate problems later in life. Engaging and easy-to-use, these books provide teens with the tools they need to thrive—at home, at school, and on into adulthood.

This series is part of the **New Harbinger Instant Help Books** imprint, founded by renowned child psychologist Lawrence Shapiro. For a complete list of books in this series, visit newharbinger.com.

how to like yourself

yourself

a teen's guide to **quieting** your **inner critic** & **building** lasting self-esteem

CHERYL M. BRADSHAW, MA

Instant Help Books
An Imprint of New Harbinger Publications, Inc.

Publisher's Note

Distributed in Canada by Raincoast Books

Copyright © 2016 by Cheryl M. Bradshaw
Instant Help Books
An Imprint of New Harbinger Publications, Inc.
5674 Shattuck Avenue
Oakland, CA 94609
www.newharbinger.com

Cover design by Amy Shoup

Acquired by Melissa Kirk

Edited by Jean Blomquist

All Rights Reserved

FSC
www.fsc.org
MIX
Paper from
responsible sources
FSC® C011935

Library of Congress Cataloging-in-Publication Data

Names: Bradshaw, Cheryl, author.
Title: How to like yourself : a teen's guide to quieting your inner critic and building lasting self-esteem / Cheryl M. Bradshaw.
Description: Oakland, CA : New Harbinger Publications, Inc., [2016] | Series: The instant help solutions series | Includes bibliographical references.
Identifiers: LCCN 2015039304| ISBN 9781626253483 (pbk. : alk. paper) | ISBN 9781626253490 (pdf e-book) | ISBN 9781626253506 (epub)
Subjects: LCSH: Self-esteem in adolescence--Juvenile literature. | Self-acceptance in adolescence--Juvenile literature.
Classification: LCC BF724.3.S36 B73 2016 | DDC 155.5/191--dc23 LC record available at http://lccn.loc.gov/2015039304

Printed in the United States of America

18   17   16

10   9   8   7   6   5   4   3   2   1   First printing

To my family, friends, and my husband, Andrew,
for their support on this journey, and to a friend
I will never forget, Daniel Arato. Without him,
this journey may have never started at all.

Contents

Welcome!   1

part 1: the past

1   The Most Important Relationship You Will Ever Have   10

2   The Mystery of Forgiveness   21

3   Personal Yield Theory: You're You for Good Reasons   30

4   Forgiveness: Once You Know Better, You Can Do Better   33

5   Accepting Yourself   38

part 2: the present

6   From Past to Present   44

7   Confident Versus Conceited: The Lies We Believe   50

8   Confidence Forever   61

9   Your Inner Critic Know-It-All (ICK!)   66

10   The Epic Battle of the ICK   71

11   Thought Traps   75

12   The Tiny Grain of Truth   84

13   Your True Inner Voice   89

14   The Epic Battle of the ICK: Starring You   97

15   Labels Are for Soup Cans   106

16   Daily Facets of You: You're a Prism   115

17   The 80–20 Rule   126

part 3: the future

18   Who Do You Want to Be?   130

19   Steps to Your True Self   140

20   Vulnerability 101   160

21   Romantic Relationships   170

22   How to Be Okay with Rejection   177

23   How to Be Yourself in a Relationship   193

     Wrapping Up   197

     References   199

Welcome!

How to Like Yourself

Oh, hey! Good choice, picking up this book. To start off, I want to hit you with this right away: you *are* likable. You are awesome. And you're actually pretty great. If you put this book down now and walk away, I hope at least those few ideas will continue to bounce around in your head. I hope they hang out there and you think about them often, at random and frequent times in the day. Now, if you do choose to keep reading, that's even better! That's because I know we can have a pretty awesome time together. And I think you'll get something real, something important, and possibly even something life changing out of this book.

So I said pretty confidently that you're likable. How do I know? Who am I to come out and say you're awesome? I don't know you. I may never know you, in fact. I mean, right now, I'm actually only typing on a computer screen. You'll buy my book anonymously online or from a cashier somewhere. We are ships passing in the night. And let's be honest, some people in life really are unlikable. But that's not you. How do I know? You picked up this book. Or Googled it. Or Facebook-searched it. Or agreed to read it after a friend or family member suggested it. However you found this book, the fact that you even started reading it means that you care. People who care? They're awesome. So that's you.

I think we're off to a good start. We've already determined you're likable! Sweet. But before we keep going, I want to tell you a couple things about me—mostly because it might feel a bit weird for you to take the advice of a total stranger. So let me help out with that. First off, I'm twenty-six years old. At least, I was when I started writing this book. So I'm pretty fresh off the "how to like yourself" stage of life. I really do get what you're going through.

I'm also a counselor. I work with students in a university setting, and we talk about all sorts of things that people just like you go through. I talk with students about things going on in their lives—tough stuff, mental health stuff, relationship stuff, and other difficulties and challenges they may need help with. So, yes, I do have a master's degree in counseling.

Now, I almost didn't tell you that because I thought you'd think this book is going to be all about boring academic stuff and that it would be dry and clinical and awful. But here is some good news—I also hate books like that. So I'm going to try really hard to make this something different. And while we're at it, here's another pretty big secret that no one likes to say out loud: counselors are just people, too. Yup, psychologists, psychotherapists, counselors…just people. With some special knowledge on this topic, so hopefully we can help with that side of things, but we are just human, too. Secret's out!

So needless to say, I'm certainly not perfect. Nor do I always get everything that I'm writing about in this book right in my own life. But I'm writing about it because I have talked to lots and lots of people about this, and I've also worked really hard to practice as much of this advice as I can. So through the wisdom I've heard from people I've worked with, and also through my own trials and errors, this book was born. It is a pretty solid collection of ideas that can help you figure out how to get from where you are now to where you want to be. Liking yourself is the first step toward really changing your life so that you can be happier, healthier, and more confident in everything you do.

Pet Peeves and Things That Make This Book Different

There are a lot of self-help books out there, so let me tell you why I thought this one needed to be written. When I walked the self-help aisles of my local bookstore, I certainly found a lot of books about loving yourself. Those books are great, but most of them pick up as if you already like yourself. They go straight for the big guns. They focus on love. If you think about any good relationship you have with a friend or significant other, what stage comes before love? *Like.* I was surprised that there weren't any books out there for the "like" stage in your relationship with yourself. This book starts at the beginning.

I also found that a majority of the books were geared toward women, and women in their late thirties and up, at that. There was nothing for the teens and twenty-somethings of the world. But this is important stuff for everyone, and especially important for us! We certainly have some different pressures and influences that need to be taken into account, so this book is for us. Now really, anyone can read this book and there's probably a little something anyone can take away, but I did write it with younger people in mind. And I think its a little easier to digest than your typical book of this topic. It is more readable, more fun, and, most importantly, it starts from the ground up.

While we're at this, let me tell you some other things that I'm hoping will make this book different than the other books that are currently out there, which will make reading this really worth your time. This starts with some of my pet peeves with other self-help books, and my motivation for making this one especially for you.

Books That Are Too Intense. There are a few things I'm going to try really hard not to do. Being too intense is the first one. I never read self-help books when I was younger because they always talked about the over-the top, lofty ideas of "loving yourself," finding inner peace, and being one with the world, and it all seemed a little too much for me. I wasn't there yet! How can you love yourself if you're not even sure that you *like* yourself?

Books That Talk Down to You. Before I started writing this, I went to the bookstore and read through parts of a bunch of self-help books. I won't lie; they seemed to contain a lot of information that's similar to what you'll find in this book, just said in different ways. (There are only so many ways to like yourself that really work, after all.) But I found that in many of the books out there, it seemed like the author was talking down to me. Like the author had all the answers, and I had none. Like if I just followed these "five simple steps" (or seven steps or ten steps . . .), my whole life would be better. Simple—duh! But because it wasn't always so simple for me, reading about how easy it was "supposed to be" actually made me feel worse. I'd read one of the suggestions, and it would seem so simple, but then I wouldn't know quite how to put that magical piece of advice into action right away. Then I'd feel like I was inadequate. Then I felt I needed to buy a second, third, or fourth book with a title like *How to Feel Better About Yourself When You Can't Seem to Do Simple Things*! So I'm going to do my best to talk about this stuff *with* you, not down to you. I may not always get it right, but I'm going to try. As you read this book, the things we're going to talk about aren't always going to be easy. I want you to know that it's okay to take some time to figure things out, and that it's normal not to be able to change things overnight. That just means you are *human* and you are *normal*. Phew! Thank goodness. I'll save writing a book for aliens another time.

Books with Invincible Authors. I also found that while reading other books, I was just envious of the authors the whole time. They all went through some "year of finding themselves" or "discovered the secret to life," and then they "found inner peace." Meanwhile, there I was, sitting on the dirty floor of the bookstore reading about these invincible people, trying not to think about the fight I just had with my friend or how in the heck I was going to get anyone to read my book when I, unlike most other self-help authors, didn't have a PhD! I felt inadequate—which was just the opposite of the intended point of the book I was sitting there reading! So I'm going to be real with you. I am *not* invincible. I am also human. Complete with faults and quirks.

On that note, here's some insider info: when authors write books, it is part of their job to seem like they have it all together. Why would you buy their book if they were a total mess? Truth time—don't be fooled! No one can get it right all the time, and everyone has to start somewhere. Including authors like me.

Books That Make This Seem Really Easy. Let's be clear—there is nothing simple about liking yourself. Even though it seems like it should be easy, it's a process—and it will take time. And simply reading about how you should "just forgive others" or how you "need to be grateful" won't always help you get there without a little more explanation and practice on how to do those things. Most of us have heard those cliché bits of advice by now, and, yes, they're true! But how do you *get* there? Since we've all heard those things before, clearly it isn't that we don't know *what* to do, it's just that we don't always know *how* to do it. We will work through those things together in this book. We'll break things down, pull them apart, make sense of them all, and then put them all back together. Whee!

Books That Are Longer Than the Bible—and Claim to Be the Same. Last but not least, I'm going to do my best to keep this short. Looking at the length of some of the books in the self-help aisle exhausted me, so I'm going to do us both a favor and hit you with only the best stuff I've got. And I'll try to keep it to the point. I also want to be clear that this book is not the *Bible of Liking Yourself,* but it is a great starting point. And once you're ready, there are lots of great follow-up books out there about loving yourself, like I mentioned. But we'll start from the beginning.

And while this really could be the first step in changing the rest of your life, simply reading this book will not instantly get you there. However, thinking about the ideas in here and doing your best to put them into practice can get you to where you want to be over time. So let's get rolling (or page turning), and take the first step toward the rest of your life!

part 1

the past

1

The Most Important Relationship You Will Ever Have

Your 24/7 Friend

Imagine you had to hang out with a friend all day, every day—waking, sleeping, and eating. Now imagine that "friend" didn't like you, and she kept calling you names, doubting your intelligence, attractiveness, skills, likability, and future potential every chance she got. She was always there, hovering around you, making you feel uncomfortable and on edge, and always chiming in with her negative opinion of you. Seriously. Picture it. Close your eyes for a second and just imagine it. Ouch! No thanks. But for so many of us, that's the voice in our heads when we don't like ourselves. So we walk around with this mean voice talking to us—a voice that seems so convincing…and generally isn't very nice to us. With a voice like this talking to us, it makes sense that we would feel insecure all the time!

Now imagine that this 24/7 friend was there supporting you instead. Imagine that she respected you, your decisions, and your intelligence. Imagine that she knew you weren't perfect, but she was okay with it. Imagine that she knew you were always doing your best and that you were working to become the greatest version of yourself that you could be. Imagine that she knew it was okay when you made mistakes and that she stood by you through tough times. Imagine that she had your back when other people called you names or questioned your intentions, because she knew that you were truly worthwhile.

Man, doesn't that sound nice! Almost like every dream relationship we'd like to have in real life! That certainly would be awesome, and maybe some of you are lucky enough to have found this support in a relationship with a friend or loved one already. But why not also have this with yourself? Since you are spending 100 percent of your time with *yourself*, this is the most important relationship you'll ever have. You are the person who is going to do everything in your life with you: from the most boring moments to the most exciting moments, you will go through it all together. You will eat every meal with yourself, you will wake up every morning with yourself, you will do every chore with yourself. You will never spend as much time with anyone else as you do with yourself, so it makes sense that you should be your own best friend! So why is liking yourself so hard, how do you overcome that difficulty, and how do you get to this awesome place of liking yourself?

Why Is Liking Yourself So Hard?

We are taught from a young age how to share, how to make friends, how to work in groups, and eventually, we are filled with information on how to "get the guy" or "get the girl." We're always hearing about how to get along with *other* people. But what about getting along with yourself? You never receive any information on your relationship with yourself—which is a bit odd, if you think about it. After all, you spend 100 percent of your time with yourself! More time than with any friend, any significant other, any boyfriend or girlfriend, or any family member. Weird, huh? So why isn't there more emphasis on how to like yourself in life?

I've got a couple ideas on that. Most of the information you have ever gotten about life likely came from your school, your religion, your parents, your relatives, other adults, or your friends. We'll talk about the school system first. Schools have their own agenda, which is to teach you how to fit into the classroom environment so you don't kill each other and so that teachers and principals can do their jobs. Their goals are to get you through school and then to prepare you for the workplace. This means that their first priority is to teach you how to work hard and to work with others. As an institution, they're not too concerned with teaching you to like yourself, as it doesn't really affect their immediate goals.

Traditional schools also have a strong focus on how you can "better yourself." Of course, this is a great goal, sure—don't get me wrong. However, the drawback to this focus is that it also trains you not to be happy with the current version of yourself. Hence, many people tend to feel dissatisfied with themselves. They think they're not good enough, because school makes them feel like they're never quite "there"—that they aren't good enough yet. This can make it hard for people to like themselves for who they are today.

We also get information about life from religion. Religion, if you follow one, tends to have a pretty good framework on things like morals, values, and many other positive beliefs.

However, from what I know of religion, it doesn't really talk about your relationship with yourself—it focuses on your relationship with a higher power or God, or focuses on your relationship with other people and society. These are great things, but your relationship with yourself cannot be overlooked, as it is the cornerstone to the strength that you often need in order to engage in the rest of these practices with your whole heart. You need to like yourself before you can extend yourself fully in the other ways that religion encourages you to do. So we still need some additional information to figure out the relationship with ourselves. If you are religious, you can always draw some of your strength from your faith and beliefs as you work through this book. If you are not, that's good too, as the relationship with yourself can be built in many different ways. So that being said, let's move on to look at the kind of information we get from parents, relatives, other adults, and our friends and how this also affects the way we feel about ourselves.

If you're like many people, your parents, relatives, other adults, and friends are your biggest influence on this subject. The trick here is that most of these people were never taught how to like themselves properly either. Even though parents and teachers might be older, they also grew up in the same system that we are in, with the same emphasis being put on getting along with others and always being "better." So they tend to encounter the same pitfalls and experience the same lack of knowledge on how to like themselves as we do, even though they are older. They are human, too! You should see the number of books on how to love yourself geared toward people in their forties and older. That should tell you something! Many people have never been taught how to like themselves, no matter what their age! And your friends, well, they are probably just as lost as you are, because no one talks about how to like yourself and what it is really all about (as we just learned), so we're all just left to muddle through it alone and in silence.

To add to the problem of figuring out how to like ourselves, a lot of the people who *have* figured out how to like themselves don't always know what they did to get there, so they don't know how to teach what they've learned to others. This information doesn't always translate easily, and can be hard to put into words.

Putting this all together, our main sources of information on life come from schools that are motivated to focus on our relationship with others; religion that focuses on our relationship with a higher power or God; parents, relatives, and other adults who were never taught how to like themselves either; and our friends who are just as lost as we are! So our information about life is sincerely lacking in the "how to like yourself" category.

And this isn't all that makes this relationship with ourselves so difficult. Let's look at some other reasons so we know what we are really up against here.

The "Everyone Is Better than Me" Syndrome

We live in a world where getting along with others is emphasized above getting along with ourselves. We also live in a world where competition and comparison is everywhere, even though people try to pretend it's not. It really is! Take school as an example. We are graded on a scale. That scale determines where we fall among our peers, and then that determines what opportunities we may have available to us for further education. What about at work? We are hired or promoted on our ability to do things better than our colleagues. And even though "everyone's a winner" medals and participation ribbons hang in almost everyone's bedroom, we are still taught that life is a competition.

Why does the environment of competition make us not like ourselves? Because it always makes us compare ourselves with others. We are taught that comparison is important to make sure that we are keeping up or doing better than other people.

Now let's think about it this way. Imagine another friend. But this friend is one who you only see during school hours or work hours. How well do you think you know him? It seems like you see him all the time. School or work is a big part of your day, so you must know this person pretty well. You've talked about all sorts of things with him—his hobbies, his weekends, his holidays, maybe even his love life. You can get to know someone pretty well in these settings. And, of course, you compare yourself with him while you're at it, because you have been encouraged to do that your whole life. And man, this friend really seems like he has it all together. You like talking to him, but somehow you always feel slightly inadequate afterward, as if you're not doing something right in your own life. His life seems really interesting, if not perfect. And you feel a bit boring, unaccomplished, or inadequate when you are around him.

So what's the deal? Is it true that everyone's life is actually better than yours? Nope. The reality is that you probably only see the parts that others want you to see. The majority of people in our lives are consciously monitoring what other people know about them, and what they show others. You do it, too! It's normal. But it confuses us when we try to check in on how we are doing in comparison. We compare someone else's filtered information to our own unfiltered information. This can be a bit of a tough situation to navigate.

Since most people don't go walking around talking about their bad gas or the terrible date they had the other night, or the fact that they are failing in school, or that they really think that nobody likes them, we receive more information about other people's successes than we do their failures. And since most people *do* talk about the parties they have, their awesome new partner, the great mark they got on a test, or the amazing vacation they have coming up, it's easy to think that we're not keeping up. This gets even more confusing because, since we are with ourselves 100 percent of the time, we *do* know every single detail of our own lives (we are the ones living it, after all). We know the good, bad, and the ugly—the full truth. And since we don't know everyone else's "full truth," we think ours must suck in comparison.

The fancy name for this is the "availability heuristic," aka, What We Hear About Most Often *Must* Be True, Right? We fall into this trap when we believe that the information we get most frequently or that we can remember most easily (the information that is most available to us) is true. For example, we all tend to think we're going to die in a plane crash every time we fly because we always hear about plane crashes on the news— even though statistically, flying is much safer than driving a car! Since no one ever reports on the thousands of planes that land safely every day, our brains switch to what information we hear about most often, and then we recall all the terrible deaths and newspaper headlines, and then think that this will happen to us, too. Our brain tricks us into thinking that what we hear about most often is most true, even though this often isn't reality.

Let's sum it all up so far. In short, life is competitive. Therefore, we compare ourselves to others. But we all project and advertise our successes more than our failures. Because our brains fall into the trap of believing what we hear about most often (instead of remembering that what others tell us is usually not the whole story), we tend to think our lives are much more boring and unfulfilling than everyone else's are. I call this the Everyone Is Better than Me syndrome. (I always wanted to make up the name of a syndrome. Life step = complete!)

So What Now?

We have traveled through some interesting ideas together and have ended up with a somewhat disappointing outcome. It seems as though we are doomed to fail in this life, since our brains trick us into believing the What We Hear About Most Often *Must* Be True, Right? trap. And, of course, no one is about to stop competing, comparing, or pretending anytime soon. So we're screwed, right? Nah, we can handle this! Here's how. It takes some learning and some practice and some time. I know, it sounds intimidating, but you can do this! You've already read this far. We'll take it one bit at a time!

Here's Why It's Worth It

So let's think about life. I know, I know, a little lofty, and I promised I wouldn't do too much of that. But let's break it down. In your life today, you have a certain set of skills, friends, and knowledge. Whatever combination you have today is due to a lot of hard work and a lot of time invested.

Let's use me as an example. One of the things I did a lot while growing up (and still do now) was horseback riding. By the time I was in seventh grade, I rode at least five days a week. That means I spent an average of five hours on a horse for probably fifty weeks of the year—that's about 250 hours a year. So rough math would work that out to at least fifteen hundred hours from seventh grade to the end of high school. That's a lot of time! It would stand to reason that this would be a large part of my identity and my skill set. It's something I'm really quite good at. (I spent a long time working to become good at it!) I even taught horseback riding lessons for about five years.

In comparison, how much time do you think the average person dedicates to learning how to like herself? Let's see…possibly a random Tuesday once a month or so while watching an inspiring YouTube video, maybe a few days around New Year's while making a resolution, and maybe just after a breakup for a week or two a year, so maybe a total of four weeks out of the year, when you add up the hours that were scattered through that time.

If you were trying to learn a new musical instrument or learn a new sport and you only practiced for the equivalent of four weeks out of the year, how good do you think you would be at it?

And that's just regarding building a skill. What about building a relationship? Think about a new friend or significant other that you're trying to get to know. If you were building that relationship, how many hours would you want to spend at it? Probably a lot more than you might dedicate to a new sport or skill.

The logic is the same when you think about the time it takes to like yourself. It is both a skill and a relationship, so it's going to need some extra time in your life. Imagine you were a new friend you really wanted to get to know. Take a moment and decide how much time each week you think would be worth dedicating to your relationship with yourself. Write it down. Circle it. Put a star next to it. Highlight it in yellow marker. Put it in your agenda, your calendar, and your smartphone. Mark it "personal appointment," and don't let anyone take away your time with yourself! Reserve some *you* time for yourself—you can start by carving out time to read this book! Make sure you protect that time with yourself, snuggle up with this book, grab your journal, maybe some hot chocolate, and hang out with the number one in your life—you!

Let the Changes Begin!

All right, I think you are convinced that this journey with yourself is worthwhile. If you've read this far, you've thought about the time and effort it might take to make some changes that will help improve your relationship with yourself and you think you'll give it a try. You're dedicated and ready to go! So it might be disappointing that I am still not getting to the "what to change" part of this book. Instead I want to talk with you about forgiveness. You might be saying, "Sorry, what? I'm lost. I didn't come here to read about forgiveness, I just wanted to learn what to do to like myself!" Well, here's what it's about. This isn't about forgiving other people in your life, it's about forgiving *yourself*. Dramatic pause...quizzical looks...

It might sound like a strange next step to take in this book, but here's why it's an important one. If you've come to a point where you are reading about how to like yourself, you're probably a bit unhappy with how things are right now. And because this book is about you, that probably means that, on some level, you feel a smidge responsible. If you feel responsible for your own unhappiness, you certainly aren't going to get anywhere with liking yourself anytime soon. So we're going to start here. We'll start with an overall conversation about forgiveness, because it applies to many different parts of life, and then we'll get into how this works into the concept of liking yourself.

2

The Mystery of Forgiveness

The Muddled Definition

To start off, let me ask you this: what comes to mind when you think of forgiveness? Most people answer something like, "Letting go of grudges and bitterness and not being angry anymore." They usually relate this to trying to forget what happened or excusing the person responsible for what happened—the old "forgive and forget" cliché. This "forgive, forget, and let go" kind of understanding is what I will refer to as the "layperson's definition of forgiveness." This can sometimes be a dangerous understanding of forgiveness, since a lot of things in life really aren't "okay" and the fact that they happened isn't just "all right." Some things in life really are terrible, and some people do awful things, up to and including physical, emotional, and sexual abuse. If you use the layperson's definition of forgiveness—forgive, forget, and let go—these actions don't deserve to be "forgiven."

Given how the layperson's definition so clearly conflicts with many real life situations, it's easy to see that forgiveness is probably one of the most commonly misunderstood concepts in modern life. To make it even more complicated, there are actually two types of forgiveness, and it's important to know the difference between them. Let's look at these two different types of forgiveness now so that we don't get stuck in less-than-useful definitions. We will also explore two examples of situations that need the different types of forgiveness. We will then break these apart so that you can figure out how to make sense of which type of forgiveness to use in different situations.

✳✳✳

Forgiveness—Type 1: Using Radical Acceptance to Regain Your Power

Use for: The Tough Stuff—When It's Not Okay

This type is for the times when someone knowingly hurts you without remorse or regret. This type can include things like physical, emotional, and sexual abuse. Bullying often falls into this category, as well as manipulation, abuse of power, and, in many circumstances, cheating and lying. We're delving into this topic of forgiveness not just to look at the idea of forgiving ourselves so that we can like ourselves, but also to figure out what forgiveness means when we think of past events in our lives that may continue to trouble us. Events from our past can be roadblocks to change, so we will break these ideas down in order to help us continue to move forward.

Forgiveness as an overall concept can probably be better understood as *acceptance*. To forgive in these types of situations—when someone knowingly has hurt you without remorse or regret—isn't necessarily to forget what happened or to say something that happened was okay, or to say that you're ready to move on if something really wasn't okay. Forgiveness is to *accept* that something happened—maybe it was crappy and terrible, and it will probably always be crappy and terrible, but it is now in the past. The idea is to stop reliving it and thinking about what you could have done differently, said differently, or what you could change if you could go back in time. Forgiveness is to accept that something happened that you cannot change, but to also simultaneously acknowledge that you have the strength to move forward in your own life despite the things that have happened to you.

You accept the wrongdoing as a fact—a really shitty fact sometimes—and then say, "You know what, dwelling on this is not changing the past—the past is frozen in time." You may never be okay with what happened, and that's completely fine. It's normal, in fact. But you have today and the rest of your days to live a life that doesn't have to depend on the bad stuff from the past. Accept that you will carry the incident and the memories with you, and that you will likely never forget what happened, but know that today is the only day that matters now. You don't "forgive" the other person by trying to forget what happened or by saying that it was "okay" that it happened, but instead you accept it as fact and also accept that anger, revenge, or resentment will not change what happened. To accept the wrongdoing as something that will now live only in the past is an important step to take so that you can move forward with what will be best for you in your future. Then you get to choose what to do in your life going forward without the past dictating your every move. You free yourself. The wrongdoing now only lives in the past, not in every moment of the present.

One of the best sayings on anger and resentment is that they are "like drinking poison and expecting the other person to die." This means that the negative energy of anger and resentment lives inside of you, not the other person. You expect this negative energy to influence the other person, but that person may only be exposed to it for short amounts of time, if at all, so it barely affects that person's life. Meanwhile, this negative energy is with *you* 100 percent of the time, which isn't good for your health or your emotions. So with this new concept of forgiveness, of radical and freeing acceptance, you can remove those toxic internal emotions of anger and resentment from your present by not drinking that poison. You can do this by focusing on your present and future, and by building yourself back up and regaining your power. You take back your control of your emotions in the present; you also choose what type of energy—negative or positive—you will expose yourself to each day. You accept that the wrongdoing is static and in the past—the memory is frozen in time and is not occurring in your present. It will stay in the past, and it will never change to become either worse or better no matter how much energy you direct at it. But—and this is a very important "but"—what happens next *is* under your control.

This is how forgiveness needs to be thought of regarding any of those truly "not okay" moments, or you really will take that pain and resentment with you into your future, and then the perpetrator wins all over again. If you don't engage in this understanding of forgiveness—of radical and freeing acceptance—that person has not only your past but also your present and your future, because you are the only one living with that poison. Build a wall between those "not okay" moments and today so that the pain or anger can't leak into your today. The incident wasn't okay, but *you* are okay. You're going to be okay. You and the event are separate in time and space, and you have the power to take back your present.

By understanding this definition of forgiveness, you can protect yourself from feeling guilty if you haven't "forgiven" the other person in the layperson's definition of that term. You don't need to feel guilty. Our society stresses forgiveness, closure, and "letting go," but the incident is with you, one way or another—it's in your memories. Because it's in your memories, you can't always get closure on the incident, and you can't just forget what happened or say that what happened was okay. When society pressures you and implies that because you haven't done those things that "there is something wrong with you," you can now shoot it right back at them: "There isn't anything wrong with me. Forgiveness is about giving myself permission to move forward without letting the memories hold me back."

It's not saying that the bad things that happened were okay. You're taking your power back, and that's where the heart of forgiveness lies. Find your power in the present by accepting that the past is in the past, and that today is yours, regardless of what may have happened to you. You are in control.

Forgiveness—Type 2: Forgiving, Forgetting, and Letting Go

Use for: Genuine Mistakes or Feelings of Remorse

Sometimes, however, there are incidents in life where someone makes a mistake and truly, sincerely apologizes for it. The person really didn't mean for it to happen. Maybe there was a misunderstanding, a lack of maturity, an unfortunate situation, information missing in communication, or something else that couldn't be helped at the time. The outcome wasn't that person's intention, and that person wants to make amends. Maybe in these cases, it really is worth embracing the layperson's definition of forgiveness by forgiving, forgetting, and letting that incident go—and by developing compassion for that person. I think we've all, at one time or another, mistakenly hurt someone, so it can be helpful to recall those incidents and to empathize when this happens for someone else—even if you are the unfortunate victim. It doesn't feel great to be on either side of this fence, and remembering how both sides of this kind of situation feel can really help you work through things.

An example of this might be when a friend says he will come to your birthday party, but then he bails right before the big night. He tells you that he forgot about his plans to go to his grandmother's place that night with his family—it completely slipped his mind. Your friend really apologizes, and he feels bad about it, but you're still hurt. Why couldn't he just plan ahead better? You're really bummed and pretty upset. You really wanted your friend to be there. Well, this would be a type of situation where the mistake is unfortunate, and the timing is terrible, but your friend didn't intend to hurt you. You're mad and you're trying to figure out how forgiveness applies here, or if it even should. Should you forgive your friend? What does that even look like? How do you do it?

Perhaps you and your friend need to have a conversation about communication and planning, where you sit down together to clear the air so you can figure out how you can both plan and communicate differently next time. But this is

26

something different from the first type of forgiveness, which is for the times when someone hurts another person knowingly. Your friend truly didn't mean to hurt you, and your friendship can recover from this. This is a time that you can use that layperson's definition of forgiveness, of forgiving, forgetting, and letting go, especially after you sit down, talk about it, and sort through how you both feel.

Now, word to the wise: don't necessarily forget the incident altogether, as some people can develop a pattern of hurting you and then asking for forgiveness repeatedly. You need to protect yourself and learn from those patterns, because you might not want people in your life who follow that pattern. Some people seem unable to see how their actions might hurt another person, possibly because they have not yet developed that skill in their lives. While there may be reasons for people to have this shortcoming in their lives, it doesn't mean you have to bear the brunt of it all the time. You may need to set some boundaries with people like this to protect yourself from constantly being hurt by them. But for people who occasionally mess up, feel bad about it, and want to make things better, you can accept their apology and forgive them. Look at their overall intentions and true character, not just the small details of the immediate situation. Look at how they handled the situation after it happened—how they spoke to you, how they tried to make amends, and how they will now work to do things differently in the future, even if they aren't perfect.

✳✳✳

These guidelines can be a good place to start when thinking about what it really means to forgive. The first type of forgiveness is to accept the incident as frozen in time and unchangeable, while focusing on taking back your present and future through your personal strength. You acknowledge that the pain and anger need to stay in the past with the incident so that your future isn't also consumed by it. The second type is to forgive, forget, and let go—to accept human flaws and unfortunate mistakes, and to instead focus on the overall intent of that person, using your empathy and remembering that sometimes we all mess up in life.

Forgiveness and You

Now that we know about the grand topic of forgiveness and how it applies in both tough situations as well as in situations of genuine mistakes, how does this apply to you liking yourself? Well, first question, are you in a type 1 or type 2 situation? In your relationship with yourself, did you knowingly hurt yourself either emotionally or physically at any point? Did you knowingly make some bad decisions without remorse or regret? If so, accept that that really sucks. It may not be okay that you did, and it's pretty crappy that it happened at some point. But that is in the past—and it is frozen there in time. Recognize that you're here now, with this book in your hands, and you're ready to make a change. Past You is not who you will be tomorrow. To get to the next step, you have to remember that those actions are in the past—but don't forget about them, because Past You will be able to teach you great things in the future. (You will also need to pay extra attention to the next chapter, Personal Yield Theory: You're You for Good Reasons. It's really going to help with the concept of forgiving yourself by learning to accept yourself—the good, the bad, and the ugly.)

If you're not in type 1, then you're probably in type 2. (Or you may be in both—lots of us are, since some actions we take are on purpose and some are by accident, and we often have enough of both to put us a bit in type 1 and a bit in type 2.) Type 2 is when you haven't been happy with yourself, but it's largely due to bad circumstances, lack of knowledge or opportunity to change, or various other factors. You really have meant to try to change, but it's been hard. You're apologetic and you're trying to make amends and make changes. Give yourself a break and try not to feel so guilty—you have had the best intentions. This stuff can be really hard. You're the metaphorical "friend" in this case who really didn't mean to hurt you and who feels genuine remorse about it. Accept the apology, and move forward with forgiveness for yourself. Be kind to yourself now and in the future.

3

Personal Yield Theory: You're You for Good Reasons

Mark This Chapter, Return Often

This is one of my favorite parts of this book—it makes me truly happy. This idea of personal yield theory can be a little bit hard to wrap your head around at first, but once you do, it can really change everything. It can change the way you see your life and other people's lives, and it can give you patience, understanding, and determination for the future. Let's get a little background on where this idea came from.

In counseling, "yield theory" was developed by Dr. Christian Conte (2013), who works largely with violent offenders and criminals. If you're a counselor in this type of work, when you find yourself talking intimately with someone who has done something that goes completely against your own values and morals, you may find it pretty tough to connect to and understand that person. It can be easy to judge that person for what she's done, which disconnects you from being able to work with her, because you don't want to connect with her on a moral level. Enter: yield theory.

I know I said I wouldn't get too theory-based, but trust me, this one is worth knowing. Here's what Dr. Conte himself says about the theory: "The underlying assumption of yield theory is this: If we lived every day as another human being—not just walked a metaphorical mile in that person's shoes, but actually had the exact same cognitive functioning, affective range, and life experiences—then we would make every single decision that that person has ever made. Every single decision."

Yield theory means, essentially, that if you were to be transported into someone else's physical body and into her life circumstances at birth, you would *be* her—and make all the decisions she ever made. You would essentially be living her life as it currently is, even if, given the person you are today, you couldn't see yourself making those same choices. Your brain as you are today might not even be able to comprehend her life and her choices because you haven't been exposed to the same pressures or experiences. This theory makes you think about what your life would be like not only if you had a different upbringing and different life circumstances, but also if you had a different body and brain to work with while you were at it.

Beyond understanding other people, this theory also applies to you in your own life. I dub this "personal yield theory." Let's get into this idea of personal yield theory a little deeper.

You are a person made up of your own set of life experiences, knowledge, skills, biology, and cognitive abilities. In every moment of your life, when faced with a crossroad, you will make a decision based on those components in that moment. Time is linear—you can only make one decision at a time. True? Yes. So at any given moment in time, whatever decision you make is the only one you could have made at that time based on all those components that make you who you are, along with the circumstances of that moment. If you had been capable of making a different decision at the time, you would have.

Think about that one for a second; it's a bit philosophical: if you could have done things differently, you would have. You did the best you could at the time with the life experiences, knowledge, skills, biology, and cognitive abilities that you had in the moment. Even if you knowingly made what you may now call a "bad decision," at the time, you had a reason for making that decision. There literally is—or was—no other option. You can only make one decision, and the one you made, you made for a reason. Otherwise you would have made a different choice.

Revisit this section a few times as you continue to read through this book. Even I come back to it often, and I'm the one who came up with it in the first place! This idea will begin to make more and more sense as you continue to explore your past, present, and future. I hope you keep thinking about it, because once you can see yourself in the light of personal yield theory, I think you'll find that your patience for yourself will grow and your ability to forgive yourself will become way easier.

4

Forgiveness: Once You Know Better, You Can Do Better

The "Hindsight Is a 20–20" Trap

Everyone knows the cliché "Hindsight is 20–20," but I don't think that most people consider what that cliché really means. The phrase means that it is easy to be knowledgeable about an event after it has already happened. It suggests that had you known something different, or had you known the outcome of the decision you were making at the time, you would have done things differently. A lot of people make "mistakes" and then say, "I should have known better." Well, what did we learn with personal yield theory? If you had known better, you would have done differently. You didn't know. Thus, you did what you did. Time is linear. Whatever happened in that moment was the only thing that could have happened, because it was the thing that *did* happen. You only knew what you knew at the time, and there is literally no changing that. No amount of wishing or looking back can change that. And that's okay.

For instance, you may have chosen to go on a date with someone who had been showing a lot of interest in you. Your friends warned you that there were rumors that this person had cheated on his last partner. However, whenever you talked to him, he seemed genuine and he was super nice to you. He even explained the situation with his last partner to you, and told you that the whole thing was basically a huge misunderstanding. You continued to see him, despite the advice from your friends, and you trusted him even when you wondered about some of the texts and phone calls that he had been getting. He explained everything about those mysterious texts and calls, and it all seemed to make sense.

However, in a few months, when you tried to surprise your partner at lunch and instead found him wrapped around somebody else's face, you were devastated. You looked back at all those incidents from the past with your partner and thought, "Man, I should have known better." And it can be tempting to think that way, once you've seen all that happened and everything becomes crystal clear! It all makes so much sense now that you know the truth. But remember, when you were dating this person, with the experience and knowledge about relationships that you had then, perhaps you did not know or understand the body language that would have revealed your partner's lies; nor did you recognize some of the signals you were getting that things weren't quite right. You had nothing else to go on at the time but what you were told, so you made the best decision you could have at the time with the knowledge that you had.

But now that the relationship is over, when you look back on everything that happened, you may be able to see a pattern, and you can pick out things that are possible warning signs for future relationships. You might decide that in the future you will listen more to the advice of friends that you trust and respect. You may decide that if you get a funny feeling in the future, you will ask for a few more key details than you did in the past. You may make note of some of the body language from your ex now that you know the times that he had for sure lied to you. You may even decide to date a different type of person in the future. Or you may just chalk it up to experience and take the next relationship as it comes, a little more resilient and a little more prepared to handle anything that may come your way. Either way, you have learned something new about yourself and others that you can take into the future with you as you face new situations.

In general, when you think that somehow you should have magically thought differently or done something different in the past, you forget that—in that moment, for some reason, at the time—that wasn't an option for you. Maybe you had limited time. Maybe you were overwhelmed with too much other information. Maybe you hadn't had any previous experience with the type of situation that you found yourself in, and so you didn't know what to expect. And then there's always the pesky fact that you aren't actually a fortune teller, even though you somehow start to think that you should have been. I know I've done that one a few times!

With personal yield theory to help explain this phenomenon, we now know that whatever it was that you decided to do, think, or say, for whatever reason at whatever moment in time, that was the "right" thing for you to do, think, or say because it was what you *did* do. There's no other option. We will learn how to make this idea work in our favor as we keep going through this book, and right now we'll put this idea together with our conversation on forgiveness.

Putting It All Together

Now you've read the background information on forgiving yourself and on personal yield theory. Here's where it all comes together.

What we know: You're looking to like yourself more; hence, you are reading this book. This likely means you're not completely happy with how things currently are. Because this topic is about you, you likely feel some responsibility for where you are right now, and you are probably feeling a bit upset with yourself, or a bit guilty. This means that you need to forgive yourself—by accepting where you are now and how you got here, and removing the guilt, shame, or disappointment that may be there with it.

How do you accept this—your past and who you are today? Personal yield theory. Remember that who you are today is made up of a combination of life experiences, knowledge, skills, biology, cognitive abilities, and everything that makes you *you*. Understand that Past You only had the resources that you had at the time. Thus, you made every decision in your past for a combination of reasons based on who you were in that moment. Therefore, the decisions you made were the only ones that you could have possibly made at that time. Otherwise, you would have made different decisions. This is because you can only make one decision at any given moment, so the one you made was therefore the only one you could have made. (I know it sounds confusing, but I think you're with me now!)

You can only do what you can do with the resources you have, after all—really! Thus, you've never actually done anything "wrong." Think about it. It's really true! You have done the best you could with what you had at the moment. Yes, there are things you may have done differently had you known differently at the time, but you didn't, so you did the best you could—or what you felt like you needed to do at the time, based on who you were in the moment. This is how you can accept who you are today and where you are today. Of course, we can all learn from the past versions of ourselves, but we will do that moving forward from today, because there is nothing we can do to change yesterday. There are only things that we can do to make the future better. Only through hindsight can there be foresight.

Now that you know how to make sense of forgiveness as you apply personal yield theory to it, you can really get started on accepting yourself—the good, the bad, and the ugly. Accepting yourself is the next big step toward liking yourself, so let's keep going. We'll put together everything that we've gone over so far—and you'll like where this goes next.

5

Accepting Yourself

Here's Where It Starts to Get Good

BAM! Nailed it. You now have honestly no reason not to accept yourself. You are doing the best you can with what you have. Let me say that again: you are doing the best you can with what you have. It's science. Or philosophy. Actually, it's a bit of both. And if you haven't achieved everything you wanted to, or done everything that you hoped to, or haven't become the person that you've wanted to be, that's okay! There's a reason for it, and you know what's even better? Things can only improve from here. Why? Because you're reading a book like this. You're filling yourself with information and skills to add to Present You so that Future You can be even better, happier, and more confident! Once you know more, you can do more with that knowledge. You are always growing and changing.

What have we learned so far? That you use your own set of life experiences, knowledge, skills, biology, and cognitive abilities—the ones that are at your disposal at any given moment—to make a decision. As you continue to add to this set, you will have more to work with when faced with future decisions. Future You will be able to do better than Past You, because you are the type of person who is working on making yourself better, more reflective, and/or more confident.

Remember—as you learn more things, the past version of you won't be affected. Sometimes you might even think things like *Man, I should have known that,* and you'll feel a bit sad about past events. But just remember—you couldn't have known it or you would have acted differently! Instead, say to yourself, *I'm glad I know that now. Future Me is going to be so pleased.* So pleased!

But Always Remember to Reflect

All this talk about personal yield theory isn't to say that you shouldn't learn from the past. There is always some room for self-reflection that can benefit Future You. I'm sure you're gathering this, but it's still worth pointing out: this isn't about ignoring responsibility if we do happen to make mistakes. Of course, even if we try our best at things, or have the best intentions, we will still make mistakes, and we'll often need to take responsibility, apologize for things, and remember to learn from what happened by reflecting on it. This is the only way that we will be able to make sure we don't make the same mistakes over and over. There is a great temptation to avoid the uncomfortable feelings of a failure or a disappointment by skipping past it and not reflecting on it, because hey, who wants to sit around and think about their failures if they don't have to? But if we don't stop and reflect, we don't learn. And if we don't learn, we are more likely to just do it again later, which doesn't help anyone, especially us.

As you reflect on things that may have not gone the way you hoped, slow down and think about the details. What happened? What was going on at the time? What were you doing, what were you thinking? Who was around? What led up to the event? What emotions were you feeling? As you think about these things, you might notice something that you missed or misunderstood at the time. Once you are able to notice these things, you can look for reasons as to why you weren't able to pick up on those things at the time, or weren't able to think about them as much as you may have needed to. You can always think about what you could maybe do differently next time, now that you know more or have seen the outcome of something. But this is only for *next* time.

Watch out that guilt or shame doesn't creep into this reflection exercise. As you take note of where you may have gone wrong in the past, watch that guilt doesn't get to come out and play, because as we know, you did the best you could at the time. You can analyze your circumstances from past events and think about what you might do differently next time, but remember that you can't change the past, so do your best to avoid wishing that you could relive something. Instead, think about how you could maybe set yourself up differently next time so that you could make a different decision if faced with a similar situation. How could you create a better outcome in the future, knowing what you know now? If you didn't know something at the time, how could you try to find out sooner in a similar situation in the future? Past You can teach Future You great things.

Personal yield theory is the fastest way to change any negative feelings you may have around guilt and shame into something positive, and to help yourself refocus on your future.

Every time you think you've done something "wrong," there is a necessary grieving period—time that you need to be sad about it—for the loss of what could have been. When something goes "wrong," and you wish you had a "do-over," you need to spend time being sad that you missed the opportunity to have had things turn out differently. These sad emotions are normal, and some of this will always be part of life.

However, if guilt and shame are added into the mix of this natural sadness, the healing process can be much slower. And that doesn't help anyone. So don't feel guilty about being human—we all make mistakes, and none of us can predict the future. You can be sad when things don't work out. Being sad is normal. Being sad is even healthy. But the secret to a better future is to accept yourself as a human who makes mistakes and to forgive yourself for that, because you are trying to do the best you can with what you have and keep that guilt and shame away. Then use your powers of self-reflection to continue to grow and to make your future better, while always remembering that who you are *today* is great, too, on this journey through life; personal yield theory says so.

Now that you know how to apply real forgiveness to yourself and to others, you have made sense of who you were through personal yield theory, and you are ready to use reflection to continue to grow and learn from each experience both past and present, you are ready to move on from the past (part 1) to the present (part 2). Onward and upward!

part 2

the present

6

From Past to Present

Who Are You Today?

Now that we've gone through the steps of accepting your past and understanding where you are today, it's time to look at who you are in the present and to work on fully understanding yourself. Only then can we begin to look forward to creating the version of yourself that you've always wanted to be. But first, we'll tackle some roadblocks to making changes. We will do this so that when we get to the making changes part of the book (later in part 2 and in part 3), it will be much easier. We'll also confront some common difficulties that people face when trying to like themselves on a day-to-day basis.

First You Have to Know Yourself

Before you can like yourself, you have to *know* yourself. So who are you? The loaded question! Can we even answer that in one book? Well, we'll at least have to try!

This question definitely calls for a list. I don't ask you to get out a pen and paper often, so I hope you'll indulge me in this exercise. I'll wait while you go grab a pen and some paper. You'll probably want about four sheets. Don't worry, I'm patient. Off you go. (Taps foot while waiting.) Did you get some? Great! Good work. If you didn't, don't worry; I can wait a little longer. This is important stuff, after all. (Waits some more.) Got it? Yay! I knew you would. That just goes to show how dedicated you are to this stuff. You even got off your comfy couch and out from under your cozy blanket, risked a family member possibly seeing you walk through the house and then tasking you with some chore like doing the dishes, and then you braved the messy desk and the age-old task of trying to find one pen, just *one* pen that works out of the slew of dead pens that you save for reasons none of us ever really understands (but we all do it!) just so you could do this super important exercise. I'm pleased!

Okay, now that you've made it through the wilderness of getting your materials, it's time for that list. I want you to write down everything that you think describes you. A list of "who you are." Write down all the words or phrases—good, bad, mundane, interesting, anything—that come to mind: daughter, dancer, good listener, caring, C student, cautious, son, pushover, football player, shy, have good friends, know how to say no, nerdy, people pleaser, procrastinator—whatever fits you. Try to make the list as long as possible. Okay, go ahead. I'll wait some more. (Waits patiently.) Writing this list should take about five minutes at least. Don't worry. I'll keep waiting. Take your time. (Waits.) Done? Okay, now try to add at least three more things. The longer and more detailed this list is, the better. Once you've added three more things, remember that you can always add to the list later if something comes to mind.

So I have some good news—all that work to get pen and paper wasn't just for one list. I actually have a couple more lists for you to make! Makes getting that pen and paper seem totally worth it, right? Like you got to secretly cash in on being able to do a few more exercises but you didn't have to get up again. Okay, two more lists—almost there! This time I want you to create a list of who you *want* to be. What are some traits or qualities that you wish you had that are fairly realistic? And by realistic I mean, don't put in anything like winning the lottery or being the next Queen of England—just stick to making a list of personal qualities, skills, talents, how you want to be in relationships, that sort of thing. You can duplicate some things on your original list of "who you are," if they apply. For instance, if you put down "caring" on your first list, and this is also something that would apply to the list for the person you want to be, you can put it down again on this list. Okay, go ahead.

Good? Great. Now on to the last list—yay! Almost there! For this one, I want you to write down a list of things you think *other* people want you to be. According to your parents, friends, partner, or "the world," write down the list of things you think you're "supposed" to be. The same rule applies; if anything from either of your previous lists should also be on this list, add it here as well. If you are an A+ student (from your first list) and this is also something you want to be (from your second list), and it's also something that others (like your parents) on your third list want you to be, then this item would appear on all three lists. Okay, go ahead. This one might take a little more brain juice. I'll wait! Tricky, right? Trying to categorize all these things? Don't worry; the outcome will be pretty interesting.

Take your time. Once you're done with this last list, you should have three lists:

1. Who you are.

2. Who you want to be.

3. Who other people want you to be (who you're "supposed" to be, according to others).

Putting It Together

Congrats on completing your first assignment! You've done so well! (I mean, I'm guessing you did well. I'm just writing this book, so I can't actually see you—but I trust you!) Hopefully, you now have some fairly long lists to work with. The longer your lists, the more insight you generally get from them.

This assignment is one of the best things you can do to help understand yourself in the present. It also helps you figure out what pressures or disappointments you might be feeling in your life, even though you aren't always sure why you're feeling them. Okay, ready to put it all together?

The theory goes like this: generally, the closer your three lists are to each other, the happier you are. For instance, if your "who you are" list is very close to your "who you want to be" list, you're laughin'. You've got a good solid sense of who you are and you've worked hard enough or been lucky enough that this also matches up with who you want to be. If these two lists are quite different, you're probably going to feel a certain sense of longing, or possibly inadequacy, because you don't feel that Present You is the person you'd really like to be.

The same approach applies when you're comparing your "who you want to be" list and your "who other people want you to be" list. If these are very different, you're going to feel pulled in opposite directions, and you might feel like you're always going to disappoint someone.

Finally, maybe when you compare your "who you are" list and "who other people want you to be" lists, they are quite different. If this is the case, you might often feel a sense of letting other people down, or sometimes you might even feel rather angry, like other people don't understand you.

Various emotions can come up as you look at these lists, but just remember—none of these emotions is wrong, and there is no "right answer" for this exercise. If your lists are close to each other, cool! If they're not, that's fine! This is just about mapping out your current location in life; there is no judgment, no "better" and no "worse." Remember personal yield theory? You are uniquely and justifiably *you* based on your life experiences, knowledge, skills, biology, and cognitive abilities. Everyone's circumstances in life are different, and this exercise should just be used to understand yourself at this current moment. That's the first step in accepting your current place in life. These lists will come in handy again in the next part of the book—The Future. Don't lose these lists—tuck them away somewhere. But also don't get rid of that pen and paper just yet.

The Liking Yourself List

With this new insight into the pressures that might be in your life, or where some of your emotions might be coming from, it's time for a little pick-me-up. This is one of my favorite exercises of all time! Grab that pen and paper again. You're going to make a list as long as you can about all the things you like about yourself. Now *wait*! There's a really big discussion we should probably have right about now before you actually start this list.

Did you, like most people I talk with about this exercise, think, *Well, that sounds really conceited and full of myself?* Did you hesitate to pull out paper and pen again because this exercise makes you seem arrogant? Does the idea of making this list make you uncomfortable? Never fear, you are not alone. I know I said forgiveness was probably one of the most misunderstood concepts of our time, but here's the second one: the intertwined concepts of modesty, confidence, and being conceited. Let's take a look at these concepts in the next chapter.

7

Confident Versus Conceited: The Lies We Believe

Getting It All Straight

We are taught to be modest and that being conceited is very wrong. And let's be honest, no one really likes people who brag about themselves all the time and consistently point out how awesome they think they are. That energy is exhausting to be around, all "look at me, look at me!" and no one likes that. So when people are faced with the idea of making a list of all their good qualities, this image pops up, and many people shy away from the idea. Super common, and it makes total sense if you're trying very hard not to be that annoying person: you avoid thinking about the things that you like about yourself so you don't end up like that person. Or, maybe you are actively thinking about the things you don't like about yourself because you want to make those things better, so you focus on them all the time instead. But here's the drawback—these reactions to avoiding thinking about your good qualities and attributes also make it very hard to have confidence in yourself.

If you pull away from celebrating the good things about yourself, this means you're probably spending most of your time thinking about the things that you *don't* like about yourself. This does not lead to being a confident person. It creates an unhelpful availability heuristic, that term we learned about at the beginning of the book that refers to What We Hear About Most Often *Must* Be True, Right? Your brain uses your most common thoughts and experiences to try to simplify things for you, so it builds a belief system based on the most common things you think about, which aren't necessarily the *truest* things. What this means is that the more you think about the things you don't like about yourself, the more you will believe them, because they are the thoughts you are most familiar with. Your brain takes them all and compiles them based on how often you think about them, and then it builds your belief systems about yourself based on these ideas. This in turn makes it way easier for your brain to think about all the negative things about yourself and much harder to remember the positive things. This most certainly will affect your mood, confidence, and self-esteem. There is a fine line between being conceited and being confident. We should probably look at this fine line a little bit closer.

The Fine Line Between Conceit and Confidence

The difference between being conceited and being confident is that when you're conceited, you tell the world all the time, loudly and rather obnoxiously, about how super fantastic you think you are, and you often exaggerate your abilities. Or you use the information about your skills or talents to make other people feel worse about themselves, like they are less than you. Or sometimes you use it to try to get a group of followers to envy you, which makes you feel important. This is being conceited.

However, when you are confident, you quietly know your strengths, talents, and self-worth, and you exist in the world with a satisfying reassurance that you are worthy and exceptional in various ways. You know that you have qualities to offer which are worthwhile and important. You step up to situations because you know you can handle them even if you're not perfect. You try new things because you're confident that you can figure things out over time even if you don't get something right away. You can fail because you know a loss doesn't make you less of a person. You know that your good qualities do not disappear just because not everything is going right. When asked what's great about you, you can speak with self-assurance about your good qualities, because you are not bragging to make others feel less than you; instead, you are sharing the truth about yourself as best you know it. And the truth can always be spoken without fear of being conceited—because this is not bragging. It is making a statement of your positive qualities, which every person has. To deny this would be to ignore a universal truth: we all have positive qualities.

So where does a lack of self-confidence come from? One possible source is how we are so often asked to self-reflect in school, sports, or other hobbies about what we could be doing better, what our goals are, or where we may still have room to grow. This type of thinking tends to skew our mindset toward the negative. We think about what we lack or what we do not have "yet." There is always an emphasis on the "yet," the thing that we are currently working toward. Knowing what we don't have "yet" can help us in creating goals, which is great for growth, but this hyperfocus on what is missing is not always great for self-esteem. Because we run into this type of thinking so frequently in our lives, thinking about what we lack all the time can also make us feel awfully inadequate. It can make us feel like we're never good enough in the present, and this can be really hard on our confidence. Thinking often about what we lack also does not give us a chance to think about our positive qualities outside of concrete accomplishments or awards.

Society's answer to this general lack of self-confidence and self-esteem has been to give everyone a prize! I don't know about you, but I have a heck of a lot of participation ribbons from track and field day at school. This is the solution that people have come up with to rebuild the self-esteem and confidence that may be lacking in our younger people: give everyone an award so that no one feels bad. However, this isn't what truly creates long-term confidence, because this temporary boost is still tied to a singular, one-time, concrete event. Concrete events expire, and we don't always win in life. Sometimes we lose. Sometimes we fail. So these little boosts are just quick fixes to create small moments of self-esteem, but they don't help us build long-term confidence and self-worth.

For long-term solutions, the answer lies in practicing "positive self-talk." This means literally talking to yourself in your head about why you are awesome, what makes you cool, why you are good at things, and what strengths you have as the person you are today. Mix this positive self-talk in with a healthy dose of self-reflection and helpful goal setting, and you've got the magic combination. We'll work at putting all that together a little later. But first, we need to build that foundation of "positive self-talk" by really focusing on all that positive stuff about you. This is why making a list like the one we are putting together right now is one of the best things you can do to start building long-term self-esteem and confidence, even though it might feel a bit weird at first!

If It Feels Weird, It Must Be Wrong— Right?

Habits, both good ones and bad ones, are tricky little things to change. If you're like most people, you probably avoid thinking or talking about your positive qualities too much in an effort to avoid being viewed as conceited, like we just talked about. Perhaps you've even been taught to do this by parents, teachers, or friends; modesty is a virtue, as they say. Perhaps you don't believe in your good qualities at this point in your life, so you focus on what you lack instead. This pattern of avoiding or discounting your positive qualities and focusing on what you don't have "yet" is likely now a habit, and you don't even think too much about it. It just happens. However, this habit is something we're going to start working to change so that your habits instead fit the true definition of confidence that we talked about earlier: you quietly know your strengths, talents, and self-worth—and that you are worthy and exceptional in various ways. And this change might feel a bit weird.

One of the roadblocks to being able to change older habits is that new things tend to feel weird to us, especially if we've done things in a certain way for many years. When things feel weird, well, we label them as "wrong." To demonstrate this, let's take a wee trip back in time.

Remember your favorite pair of sneakers as a child? The ones you wore everywhere, got grass stains on, and wore until you had one of those toe-flappy shoe-mouth things going on? And you made that toe-flappy shoe-mouth talk to your friends? (C'mon now, we all did it!) Those shoes were the best! You loved those shoes. But once the toe-flappy shoe-mouth appeared, you knew it was time; they had to be replaced. They no longer worked anymore. You didn't want to give them up, but your parents had seen the toe-flappy shoe-mouth and knew they were now officially broken. They had to be replaced and there was no turning back.

Then you were dragged out to the mall or department store to buy new shoes, and, of course, your mother or father or who-ever you were with insisted you buy your new shoes with "a little room to grow." So you did your best to pick out a new, cool pair of sneakers, but as you walked around in the store in them, they just felt *weird*. And this probably made you think again about your old favorite pair of shoes and how sad you were that you had to part with them.

After buying the new shoes that you talked yourself into liking—so much so that you even wore them out of the store!—you still looked forlornly at your old shoes sitting in the mall garbage can, after your parents had quickly decided when leaving the store that those old shoes needed to hit the trash *now*. You tried to tell yourself that your new shoes would be just as good as your old ones, maybe even better, but you just didn't believe it at the time. As you sadly plodded through the mall toward the car, every step in your new shoes felt a little bizarre and a little too roomy. You couldn't stop thinking about how these shoes just weren't as good as your old ones and that they'd never feel right. If you could, you'd have kept your old shoes just a little bit longer.

Brings a tear to the eye to remember it, am I right? Okay, so maybe that's a little dramatic, but you get the idea. Because what happened next? About two or three weeks later, your new shoes were nice and worn in, your feet got used to the new sensation of the different shape of the shoes, and you grew into them a little. Then you realized that, hey, these shoes didn't smell as bad as your old ones, they were clean, and when you stepped in a puddle, you didn't get a sock full of water. Maybe new shoes had some benefits after all!

And that, ladies and gentleman, is your metaphor for letting go of old habits and trying new ones. Even though it might feel weird at first and it can make you sad to give up comfortable old habits, or even if it feels a little scary, with a little patience, and if you hold on long enough, you'll get used to how something new feels. You might even see that it works better than what you were doing before. For instance, if you try out positive thinking in your head and think, as you shudder, *This is weird. This feels all strange and unusual, and it just doesn't feel like me!* Well, that's because you're so used to your old pair of shoes—your old way of doing things. Of course something new will feel a bit odd! But keep at it—eventually that new weird feeling fades away and you realize that positive thinking actually can be pretty useful, and it only felt weird because you hadn't practiced it before. If the shoe fits, wear it, as they say! Try on some new shoes and keep wearing them for a while until they start to feel comfortable. You might surprise yourself!

Old Habits Die Hard

Okay, one more example to help you understand how hard changing old habits can be, but also that it's possible! What we are really talking about here is something called *neuroplasticity*, the ability of your brain (your neurons) to change as you mold and shape your habits over time. Your brain is rebuilding little connections and pathways as you work to change habits or learn new skills.

So what I want you to try right now is to cross your arms for me. Yup, just cross your arms as you normally would. Don't think about it. Okay, now look down at your arms. Which arm is on top? The left or the right? I know for me, my left arm likes to be on top, with my right hand tucked up underneath my left. Okay, now shake out your arms. Now I want you to try crossing your arms the other way. Try it! That means whatever arm was on top last time is going to be on the bottom this time. For me, when I switch my arms, my right arm is now on top, with my left hand tucked up underneath.

Here's what usually happens: when you go to cross your arms opposite from how you normally cross them, your brain has to slow down and really think about what to do. It takes a lot more effort. You can't really do much else at the same time because your brain has to focus on figuring out this new task. When you cross your arms like you usually do, you do it quickly, without thinking, and usually can continue doing whatever other task you were already doing. When you change a habit like this and do it in a new way, you can actually feel your brain struggling to figure things out. It takes longer and it feels really weird. Even once you manage to figure out how to cross your arms the other way, with the other arm on top, it then feels bizarre to hold that position.

However, if you were to cross your arms this "other way" every day for a week or two, your brain would settle down and it wouldn't feel so weird. It wouldn't take so long, and it would start to feel normal. The tough part is getting through that "weird feeling" phase as your brain reorganizes itself. But change does happen! Everything you have ever learned is a result of neuroplasticity, so let's use it to our benefit this time.

Making the Best List Ever

Okay, hopefully you are with me now about the importance of really sitting down and thinking about all the awesome stuff about you, even if it feels a bit weird. It's time to make that list! Pull out that pen and paper again and start to write down all the things you like about yourself. Anything and everything! Smart, compassionate, nice hair, fast learner, good at basketball, good friends, good at computer games, determined, thoughtful, creative, loyal—whatever applies! Get into the tiny details. If one of the things you like about yourself is that you're rarely sick—sure! You like your nail beds? Awesome! Think about your physical, mental, and emotional qualities—and your relationships, skills, talents, and passions. Even pull out a thesaurus if you want! Try to make this list as long as you can! If your list isn't very long, let me reassure you that it's not because there are not a lot of great things about you; it's largely due to the fact that you're probably out of practice at thinking about your strengths. It can be really hard to bring things up in your memory that are positive if you don't do this exercise very often.

So don't worry! The list will grow as you continue to practice positive self-talk; I've seen it happen many times. Okay, off you go! I'll be waiting, as usual. (Waits.) Take your time! This list is super important. (Waits.) Okay, now add at least three more things. (Waits.) Sweet. Good work!

And How Did It Feel?

Did it feel a bit weird to make a positive list? If yes, that's okay. As we mentioned with the shoe metaphor, and with the arm-crossing exercise, that's actually normal. It will take some practice, the same way that learning any new skill takes practice. If it didn't feel too weird, that's a great place to start from! Whichever place you're at, continue to add to your list as often as you can, whenever you think of something over the next couple days, weeks, even months. This list is truly important—it is the starting place for real confidence. You ideally want to be able to mentally scroll through this list of positive qualities at any given moment. The goal is to be able, at some point, to have this list come to mind quickly and easily, without hesitation. Then, when you have times that you're feeling a bit less sure of yourself or anxious about something, this is your go-to place in your head to talk to yourself and use that "positive self-talk." You can use it to boost your confidence when you try something new or take a new risk, because you will remind yourself that even if you happen to fail, it's okay. You've got so much other great stuff about you! You've got this whole list that is yours and it won't change, even if you take a risk and it doesn't work out! This list is yours to own.

Take your list and keep it with you always. Some people I know have written it on a little note and kept it their wallet or purse, some people type it as a note on their phone, some print it out and post it next to their bed, and some have it next to their computers. You can also download the app that accompanies this book, PositiveU, to keep track of your positive list. Whenever you are feeling down or unsure of yourself and you can't pull up the list mentally, grab the physical or virtual copy of the list, however you choose to record your information. Read it often to refresh your memory so that it becomes easier and easier to recall even in hard times, because what we are really after is longevity, which is what we will talk about next.

8

Confidence Forever

Making It Last

Now you have a list of all the good things about yourself. This is a great start. But we also need to talk about longevity here. This book, after all, isn't meant to help you like yourself just for today. That's what those inspirational pins on Pinterest are for—a quick pick-me-up! But those don't really last for the long haul. That's why you've invested your time in reading this book instead, because this change is going to be for good. It's going to be *forever*! I want to help you figure out how to take the steps toward liking yourself that are going to last, and how to take steps that are going to feel honest, real, and true so that you never have to question or doubt your relationship with yourself again.

So the next questions are these: What do you want to like yourself for? What do you want other people to like you for? A lot of people think about things like fame, importance, or being relevant. Some people think about money, or being trendy or cool. Some people want others to look up to them, or even envy them, as they have so often envied others in the past. There are lots of different reasons we like to be recognized in society, and some of these can be really nice. Was one of these your main answer? If so, that's not unusual, but I also want to talk with you about why that might be a tricky road to follow. Not impossible, but tricky. And here's why.

Consider this hypothetical list of reasons that someone might like herself. Maybe she's the funniest person she knows, she has a good part-time job, she gets good grades, and has a loving boyfriend. The problem is, her reasons for liking herself are based on the ways that she's recognized by others, who see her as the funniest person around, the one with the best part-time job, an awesome student, and having a perfect romantic relationship. So tell me this: What if someone comes along and joins her circle of friends in a few months who is funnier than she is? What if she loses that part-time job? What if she has to take a course in school that she really struggles with and gets a much lower mark than usual, or what if she fails? What if she breaks up with her boyfriend? What reasons does she now have to like herself?

It is very important as you look at reasons for liking yourself that those reasons can last *forever*—not just until something goes wrong. This is done by making sure you have a solid foundation of liking yourself rooted in things that you can control. If all the reasons you listed for liking yourself (your friends, family, job, grades, and so on) are outside of your control (things that can change at any time), you put yourself at risk when the tides change in life. And they always do.

If you instead answered my original question of why you want to like yourself and why you want others to like you with

"Because I am a genuinely nice person worth getting to know," that will probably be easier. It will keep you a lot more stable over time and through the ups and downs of life.

You want to dig deep and make sure you have a good set of reasons why you are worthwhile as a human being—just for being you—and these reasons need to be within your control and yours alone. Things like being a nice person, and being caring, compassionate, and understanding. Things like having certain skills or knowledge, and having interests and passions. These are the types of things that no one and no situation can take away from you. Make sure you have some items like this on your list, for sure!

Now this doesn't mean you shouldn't celebrate the external qualities that you have or the temporary situations that you are in as well, because they are a truly awesome addition to your list. You just want to make sure that you have a solid foundation of things that aren't dependent on other people or situations. Because without these *you* things, it can get pretty tough to make it through the hard times in life when external things change (breakups, bad marks in school, job losses, fights, and so on).

To sum up, to truly like yourself in a real, long-term kind of way, essentially you want to value your internal qualities the most. These are qualities such as being nice, supportive, understanding, patient, honest, brave, friendly, genuine, passionate, interesting, skilled, caring, trustworthy, outgoing, creative, thoughtful, intelligent, reflective, loyal, compassionate, empathetic, and so on. You may have listed some qualities that I've missed—look for the items from your list that are *all you*— the ones that no one can change except for you. These are the things that will make liking yourself last the long haul. No one can take these qualities away from you, and you will always be worthwhile, no matter what state your external circumstances might be in. You will always have *you*, and you will respect and like yourself for the best kind of reasons. Not only will people want to be around you if you have qualities like these, *you* will want to be around you.

Do unto Others, but Also to Yourself

So we just learned that it's important to have, develop, and maintain personal qualities that are within your control. What's nice about this is that these qualities will help other people want to be around you as well, and for the right reasons—because you are truly caring and nice to others—and this in turn can boost your self-esteem and help you to like yourself even more.

However, just having other people like you and want to be around you isn't always a guarantee that you'll like yourself. There are plenty of seemingly popular people who actually have a lot of trouble liking themselves. They appear well-liked, surrounded by other people, and they are usually quite bubbly and chatty in social situations. However, some people who seem like this on the outside live a bit of a different life on the inside. Some, when by themselves, aren't very happy, and they don't like spending time with themselves. Maybe you are one of these people. This is because having other people like you isn't going to make you happy if you don't like yourself or if you aren't nice to yourself. So while finding ways to be nice, caring, and compassionate to others is a wonderful first step, the next step to really liking yourself is to be truly nice, caring, and compassionate to *yourself.*

Strange concept, I know. It seems that way to us because, as we talked about before, there's not a lot of emphasis on being nice to yourself in life. In school, we learn how to share with others, how to cooperate in groups, and how to be nice to our peers, but no one talks about being nice to ourselves. And again, all those pesky comparisons we have to make and future goals we are forever asked to set often train us to be pretty hard on ourselves in our own head. We can feel like we're never quite good enough as we currently are. This is when we develop a critical inner voice—our very own Inner Critic. Everyone has one. We're going to learn a lot about this fellow, the Inner Critic. Let's start to get you acquainted with your own. In order to get deep down into liking yourself, your Inner Critic has to take a backseat. This is what we'll look at next.

9

Your Inner Critic Know-It-All (ICK!)

Roadblocks to Liking Yourself

The first thing to know is that we all have an Inner Critic, no matter who we are. Bill Gates, Taylor Swift, Emma Watson, Ryan Gosling, and the President all have one. We should probably get on a first-name basis with this Inner Critic thing, so how 'bout we give it a name? The Inner Critic Know-It-All—because that's usually how it sounds in our heads, like it somehow always knows best and always knows better than we ever do. It's a bully, and it is always telling us we are wrong or what we should be doing differently. We will thus dub this terrible little creature the ICK. Fitting acronym, I think. ICKy, indeed!

Okay, now that the secret is out that we all have one of these nasty little ICKs, you don't have to feel like there's something wrong with you because you have this other voice in your head. In fact, there is actually a very good reason that we, as humans, have an ICK—it has actually helped the human race to become as productive as we are today. Think about it. If people in history had never had a little inner voice that questioned them or pushed them to be better and to do more, we would probably all still be hanging out in our caves with our fur loincloths and stone tools. But as humans, we weren't satisfied with that. Those of us who prospered best in society had a little voice telling us to try harder, be better, and to achieve more. The humans in history who had this critical voice then survived more often, had more babies, and passed their genes down to their offspring—ICKy voice and all. And this has produced great things from—and for—humanity. Look at us now! You might even be reading this book on a fancy e-reader or tablet right now! We wouldn't have these things as humans if we didn't develop a critical inner voice that made us always try to be better. But, like many things over time, the ICK can shift away from its intended purpose and take over. Instead of helping to balance us, it can become the strongest voice in our heads, becoming an overbearing bully, and then we get lost to its defeating power. The real trick is to find a balanced relationship with this voice and cut it back down to size. How? Let's take a look at that next.

Let's just put it all out on the table. Something talks to us inside our heads, and it isn't always so helpful. In fact, sometimes it's downright horrible and debilitating. It's mean. It's cruel. That's the ICK—our nasty little mental companion that always has a front row seat to our life, and always has something to say. It doesn't just point out what you might be doing wrong or could be doing better, but it tears you down as it does this. It tells you that you aren't good enough, and that you'll never be good enough. It takes "being hard on yourself" to a whole new level.

The ICK in your head takes different shapes or forms for different people. I want you to take a moment right now and think about what yours is like. I want you to picture the tone that your ICK has, the mood it has, the words it uses, and what it might look like physically, if it were to come to life. If you're feeling really keen and artistic, it may even help to draw a picture of your ICK. Close your eyes and imagine it. What does yours look like?

Some people will tell me that their ICK looks like a coach or teacher that they've had. Some people think of a parent or family member. Some people think of a different version of themselves, dressed differently or speaking differently. Some people imagine someone they've never really met, but that most of us would recognize as a character from a movie, like a mean high school cheerleader, or a tall man in a suit, or a police officer. Some people don't picture a person at all, but think of a big dark cloud, or a tornado swirling around in their head. Some people just think of a color, like the color gray pressing in on them. There is no right answer, and everyone's ICK is a little different.

Now take a moment to think of what your ICK usually says. Most ICKs seem to have common catchphrases they use a lot. Think for a second, and then write down a few of your ICK's favorite phrases. Here are some examples that people have told me their ICK says: "You're worthless," "You shouldn't say that, it's stupid," "You know no one likes you anyway," or "Why do you always have to mess everything up?" Your ICK may have some expressions like these. There will probably also be many others that are unique to your particular ICK. If you have something that you hear in your head a lot that is decidedly *not* uplifting, you can probably attribute it to your ICK. Take a moment and tune into these catchphrases. In fact, let's write a few of these down. Grab a pen and paper and see if you can identify some of the things your ICK usually says. Make a list. This will be helpful to look back on as we start to separate out the ICK from your True Inner Voice in the next few sections.

Once you have a few written down, or as many as you can think of, keep reading. Next we'll learn more about this ICKy character.

Watch Out, the ICK's Tricky

One thing to watch out for is if your ICK sounds like "I can't do anything right" or "I'm never going to amount to anything." Notice any difference between these phrases here and the last few examples of common ICK catchphrases that I gave in the last section? Same theme, slightly different tone—but in the examples I gave in the last section, the ICK was talking *to* you. Check it out again: *"you're* worthless." In the examples just given above, it's as if you are talking to yourself: *"I* can't do anything right." The examples in this section here both started with "I" instead of "you."

The ICK is a bit more difficult to deal with when it talks to you in the first person—starting the sentences with "I"—because we are a whole lot more likely to believe ourselves than someone else. Think about it. Imagine you were talking to yourself in your head and you said, *I need to get out of this building, it's on fire!* and then you had to stop and think, *Hmm, is that my real inner voice? Should I trust it? Should I get out of this building, or should I try to figure out if that statement is true or not?* Well, you just might find yourself stuck inside a burning building while you try to figure that out. So you *do* need an inner voice that you can listen to pretty quickly at times when you need it. You can't be questioning yourself all the time. That's why you need a way to determine the difference between your True Inner Voice and your ICK. The True Inner Voice is the one that will tell you what is true and helpful, and will get you out of any burning buildings when there really is a fire. You do have to be able to trust yourself and what you say to yourself, so we have to remove the ICK's ability to take over your inner voice. The ICK can't be allowed to use the first person when it is trying to berate you for something.

You need to reserve the right to speak to yourself in the first person in a way that can be trusted and is helpful. For instance, at some times in life, you may have the thought *I am sad right now.* You have to be able to be honest with yourself about what you think and feel, and to be able to trust these thoughts as you have them. So when the ICK sneaks in and tries to take over that True Inner Voice by adding on its own fun version of torture—for instance, *I am sad right now; I'll always be sad and I don't deserve to be happy, why do I even bother trying?*—here's where we need to draw the line. The ICK lies. It makes things seem worse than they really are, and it does this in some pretty sneaky ways. We'll look at all these sneaky ways a little later in the Thought Traps chapter, but first I want to share a simple tool to keep the ICK from disguising itself as your True Inner Voice and trying to pretend it's the real you. It's time to start the battle of a lifetime, and get the ICK against the ropes. Let's look at how to do that.

10

The Epic Battle of the ICK

Five Steps to Victory

Now that we have a proper introduction to the little ICK that lives in our heads, and we know a little more about this character, we're going to go through five easy steps to defeat this bully. We'll go over two of these steps in this chapter; one of the steps in the next chapter, which is called Thought Traps; and the last two steps you will find in the upcoming chapter called Your True Inner Voice. The steps are spread out at first so that we really and fully understand each part of what is involved in each step, and once we get that under our belts, then we will put all the steps together for one clean, uninterrupted battle to your personal victory over your nastly little ICK. Let's get started on learning step 1!

Step 1: Change "I" to "You"

When your ICK takes hurtful sayings and makes them sound like your True Inner Voice by using the pronoun "I" instead of "you," it takes your personal power and uses it against you. It appears to be your True Inner Voice, but it takes that voice and warps it into something far worse. This is how the ICK tries to trick you, but you can take that power back. So if your ICK currently likes to use "I" when it talks to you, use step 1: change "I" to "you." Not everyone's ICK uses "I," but if yours does, start here. You can check back to some of the ICK catchphrases you just wrote down and see if they start with "I" or "you."

If you hear your ICK using a statement that starts with "I," simply notice this, stop for a second, and rephrase it with a "you." You'll know it is your ICK talking instead of your True Inner Voice because it will be overexaggerated, unfair, and usually mean or defeating. It will sound like a bully might sound to you. So if the ICK says, *I'm a terrible person*, stop, think, *Huh, I need to change that*, and then say, *You're a terrible person*. I know that doesn't seem like much right now, because that's still a pretty mean thing to be saying to yourself, but this is the first step needed before you can really tackle that ICK once and for all. This will help create some distance from what the ICK is saying so you can break it down and battle it out. Once you've mastered this step, you can get into the ring with the ICK and start to win this fight.

Step 2: Visualize the Gremlin

Now that you've been able to distance your ICK from your True Inner Voice by changing "I" to "you," we're going to make the ICK truly icky in every way possible. If your ICK always spoke to you with the pronoun "you"—for instance, *You will never be good enough*—you will start your battle with the ICK from here.

So now we need a visualization for this step. We are going to take away some more of the ICK's power by showing it for what it really is.

I originally asked you what your ICK looked like to you—maybe your image was of a parent, teacher, friend, an alternate version of yourself, or some other character. I want you to think of that image again now, and then I want you to take that image and throw it out the window. Seriously, imagine a real window, and then visualize flinging your original image out into the wind. See it floating away, arms flailing as it swirls into the distance. Try it! Add some sound effects! "Wheee!" Doesn't that feel better?!?

Okay, so what image do you use instead? What does the real ICK look like? It doesn't get to look like something intimidating or powerful. That's a trick. So instead, have you ever seen one of those commercials for cough medicine with the little green mucus men that live in your lungs? A small, ugly, slimy green creature with a raspy, silly voice? Picture that. That's your new ICK. Or something like it. I like to call it the "gremlin." This gremlin is now the new image of your ICK—the other one was a disguise used to intimidate you. Tricky. That was a ploy to make you feel bullied into believing everything it told you. This image swap helps you see the ICK for what it really is—ugly, mean, tricky, and slimy. Shrink it down to size and see it for what it really is so you can take your power back!

Okay, let's do a little review. Step 1 was change "I" to "you," and step 2 is visualize the gremlin. (Don't worry; we will recap all the steps at the end.) So go ahead now, visualize the gremlin and hear those catchphrases coming out of the gremlin's mouth instead of from the mouth of your original ICK image. Picture the gremlin standing there, shaking its little slimy green arm at you as it talks: *You're no good, you're worthless, and you'll never amount to anything.* Picture it! Ha! Ha Ha! Really?! It's just funny now! Who is this little gross bully to tell you what you can and cannot do? Exactly. There lies the true face of your Inner Critic, and now that you can see it clearly, it's time to really take back your control.

11

Thought Traps

Step 3: Catch the Thought Traps

Now that you have some real understanding of the main antagonist here (the bad guy in the movie—the ICK), you, the protagonist (the good guy) need to know a few more things to finish off the job. This requires an understanding of some of the tricks the ICK has up its sleeve (its gross, mucus-y sleeve), which we will call "thought traps" (or, in fancy clinical terms, "cognitive distortions"). We'll call these thought traps because that's exactly what happens: you're going along, living your life, then—BAM!—the ICK throws one of these thoughts your way and you just get trapped in it. These thoughts bog you down, and it can be really hard to find your way back out of them. They trap you with how real they seem at the time. The ICK uses thought traps to make you think things are worse than they actually are. Let's look at a few of these tricks up close. We will now go through several categories of these thought traps and as we do, we will thoroughly learn how to take step 3: catch the thought traps. It's time to arm yourself with information so you can come out on top in this epic battle of the century!

All-or-Nothing Thinking: I'm Perfect or I'm a Failure

Remember that time you got two goals in that game of soccer, but because your team still lost, you felt like you played horribly? How about the time you got a really good grade on that math test, but all you remember is how you lost points because you forgot a couple of negative signs? What about the time your music teacher applauded your performance in front of the whole class, but then mentioned one little mistake you made, and that was all you could think about for the rest of the day? The all-or-nothing trick is one that the ICK uses to keep you focused on your failures and to forget the accomplishments you've made when something isn't completely perfect. When one thing isn't going right, all-or-nothing thinking makes you fixate on the negative. It keeps you from celebrating your accomplishments, which keeps your self-esteem low. The lower your self-esteem is, the more power the ICK has, and that's how it tends to like it—it does everything it can to keep you at your lowest.

Overgeneralization: If One Thing Sucks, Everything Sucks Forever

Remember that one time when you finally worked up the courage to ask out that girl, and even though she was nice about it, she still rejected you? You walked away thinking, *Man, no one is ever going to like me and I'm going to be single forever.* What's that, you say? Overgeneralization. This is when you believe one negative event is a pattern that will last forever and will never get better. Not true! Just because something happened once, or even a few times, it doesn't mean it's going to be that way forever. Maybe this was even the third or fourth rejection in a row, but hey, it happens to the best of us, and it doesn't mean things will be that way for all time.

The ICK uses this trap to keep your self-esteem low by making you feel like you're doomed instead of allowing you to face new situations with a fresh, positive outlook regardless of negative past events. When you imagine that negative events are a never-ending pattern, you're less likely to take chances in life with confidence. This causes you to miss out on opportunities to build new, positive memories about yourself. Those missed opportunities could have helped you build your self-esteem. When you miss opportunities or you go into new situations with low confidence, you likely won't do as well as you could have if you had felt better about yourself. This perpetuates the cycle—you don't do well, so you feel like a failure, and because you feel like a failure, you don't do well—just like the ICK wants. Again, the ICK gets to stay in power in this situation.

Disqualifying the Positive: That Didn't Count Anyway

You are lamenting one day to your cousin, "Man, I don't have any good friends!" and she pipes up and says, "Well, you've got me!" and you say, "Yeah, but you don't really count, I mean, you're great, but you're also family—you *have* to like me." So your cousin tries again (because she really is a good friend) and says, "Well, what about Nisha?" and you say, "No, she doesn't count, I've known her like forever. She's been in my life so long that she's almost like a sister." Suddenly you now feel all alone with no friends, even though you have, at the very least in this example, two awesome friends that you just mentioned, but you managed to discount them for weird reasons! Plus you've probably bummed out your poor cousin who was just trying to cheer you up. The ICK made you find reasons that these friends "didn't count." And the reasons they didn't count were bogus— they were made up by your ICK to keep you feeling alone. By finding excuses that the positive experiences you have "don't count" for some reason or another, your ICK keeps you believing the lie that there are only negative things in your life.

Jumping to Conclusions: Of Course I'm Right

Have you ever thought about trying something new and then said to yourself, *Well, that's a bad idea, I'm just going to fail anyway.* Interesting! How did you know that? That's like being able to tell the future! Perhaps you have a calling in life to be a fortune-teller!

And what about that time when you didn't want to go up and meet that new person, because you just *knew* she wouldn't like you and that she was already thinking negative things about you? Huh! Cool! You can also read minds! The circus would love you! These subgroups of the category of jumping to conclusions are called the "fortune-teller error" and "mind reading," respectively. These are perfect career paths for the ICK to try at the circus one day, but they aren't for you. Don't worry—we'll explore these thought traps a little more now so you can outsmart that ICK!

Fortune-Teller Error

With the fortune-teller error, the ICK makes you think something is not going to work out, so you might as well not even try. It keeps you from remembering that if you don't try something, you are *sure* to fail, whereas if you at least try, you immediately have a much greater chance of succeeding. Also, this thought trap keeps you from remembering that even if you do fail at something, all is not lost because you will at least have learned something along the way, and you never know where that may lead you. The fortune-teller error traps you by making you anticipate that things will turn out badly, and then it makes you feel convinced that your prediction is an already established fact. You are sure there is no point in trying because you already feel that you know the outcome. This then keeps you from disproving the ICK's theories (isn't that handy for the ICK?), so the ICK makes you think that it was probably right all along and that it was best that you didn't try after all. Sometimes this can even make you feel like your ICK kept you safe, which can lead you to trust your ICK (watch out, it's a trap!). This can be especially dangerous—when that negative voice starts to feel like a safety blanket.

Also, these negative predictions that the ICK puts in your head can make you doubt yourself so much that even when you do try new things, it actually *is* hard to be successful because you're so focused on the negative possibilities. This drops your self-esteem even lower, because now you've proven the ICK's negative prediction to be completely true. You think that it was right and that you are actually terrible at all new things—without realizing that you never even got a fair chance to prove the ICK wrong in the first place. The ICK drops you to your lowest, and then it sends you out in the field to fail. Again, this makes you think that your ICK was actually right all along, and you end up falling into the trap of trusting the ICK. You feel if you had just listened to "your gut," you never would have gotten embarrassed. You start to feel that strong connection with your ICK—that it would have protected you. Don't trust it! It's setting you up for failure.

Mind Reading

With mind reading, you somehow "know" what another person thinks or is going to think, without ever having this suspicion confirmed. You randomly conclude that someone is reacting negatively to you, and you don't bother to check this out. The ICK does this to strip away your confidence. This is because when you feel like you already know what the other person thinks, and that those thoughts are negative, you don't want to talk to that person in case the fear is true. You avoid ever finding out so that you can stay "on the safe side," in case the ICK is right. This leaves you walking around truly believing that other people don't like you, or that they think bad things about you, because the ICK keeps you from ever disproving these thoughts. The truth is that most of these mind-reading moments are quite likely not true at all. Most people are too wrapped up in their own world to actively direct negative thoughts toward you!

Catastrophizing: It's the End of the World!

This one is pretty easy. You failed one English quiz worth 5 percent of your overall grade, so you're going to fail the whole course! You missed a move in your dance recital? Everybody saw it and will think you're a horrible dancer, and no one will ever want to be your friend! How is that even related? Yet the ICK does it! Time and time again! You didn't get into your number one college choice? You will be homeless on the street by the age of twenty-five! Clearly, the ICK does this one to scare the crap out of you. When you're scared and overreacting, it's hard to feel good about yourself and feel positive about how your life is going to turn out. But when you look back on these situations, sometimes they're actually pretty funny. Write some down—they make good stories to tell yourself once you can truly see the ICK for what it is and know the tricks that it plays. A good laugh will be had by all.

Emotional Reasoning: I'm Sad, So Life Sucks

When you have a bad day, everything seems worse. Your friends don't seem as nice to you, your parents are horribly strict and overbearing, you never seem to catch any breaks, that kid in gym class really does hate you, your partner doesn't really appreciate you—and the list goes on. You assume that your negative emotions reflect the way things really are: "I feel it, therefore it must be true." The ICK is great at making you believe that your emotions reflect the way the world really is (with 100 percent accuracy), which is a great way to trick you out of remembering to be rational and remembering that "this too shall pass." A lot of people make some pretty bad decisions on bad days—decisions such as leaving a job, saying things to people that maybe they don't really mean, ending a relationship, or dropping out of school because of some intense negative emotions at the time. Challenge the ICK and give yourself some room to think, reminding yourself that emotions can't always be trusted in the moment. Give it some time and revisit your concerns once the ICK doesn't have as strong of a hold on you.

"Should" Statements: The Hardest One to Catch

This is a tricky one to beat, because sometimes, "should" statements seem pretty useful. "I should do my homework," "I should eat healthier," and "I should exercise more." All true, probably! So it's hard to see this as a bad thing. This is one of the ICK's best tricks, because it is so easily disguised. The trouble with "shoulds" (or "shouldn'ts") in life, even when they are true, is how they are presented to you. The ICK presents these could-be positive statements to you in a way that simply makes you feel guilty because you aren't currently doing "that thing," whatever it is. Then you feel badly about yourself and actually end up feeling less motivated. This drains your energy and makes you less productive, which once again eats at your self-esteem.

The best way to deal with "shoulds" is to use statements that instead instill a sense of positivity, such as "I'm going to work on eating better" or "In fifteen minutes, I'm going to start my homework." Other great replacements for "I should" are "I get to…," "I can…," "I'm going to…," "I plan to…," or "I want to…" These simple changes can empower and motivate you to do things, instead of making you feel guilty and forced to do things against your will. These replacements also give you more concrete goals instead of a vague sense of not being good enough.

Now that you know a bit more about the different types of thought traps, you will have a much easier time catching them when they happen. But to make matters even more difficult, there's another reason thought traps are so challenging to deal with. Let's look at why, and what you can do about it.

12

The Tiny Grain of Truth

Why Thought Traps Are So Tricky

The ICK has something really powerful on its side here: the tiny grain of truth. In almost all of the thought traps (especially catastrophizing and jumping to conclusions), the ICK will use the tiny grain of truth against you. Everything is always a possibility in life, and nothing is guaranteed, neither the good outcomes nor the negative outcomes. Is it possible that the person who just seemed to look at you funny thinks you are a horrible person? Yup, that's possible. How likely is it? Probably not very likely. But because the ICK takes that tiny grain of truth that we all know is a possibility in life and then it makes us think it's really, really likely, and because this usually plays on our vulnerabilities and fears, this can make it very hard to argue with the ICK. Because what if the ICK is right?

Follow the Fear: Change "What If" to "I Can"

This is where the self-esteem that you've been building comes into play. What if the ICK is right? What if that random person *does* think you're a horrible person? Who is he, anyway? And even if he does think that about you, what could you do about it?

When the ICK presents you with a fear—a big "what if...?"—you need to change it to an "I can..." So *what if* that person really does think you're horrible? What can you do about it? You can do many things, including ignoring him or talking to him. Let's say you follow that fear, that "what if" and you end up deciding, "I *can* go talk to him so he can learn who I really am." Now the ICK throws another fear—and another and another—at you.

ICK: What if that doesn't work? What can you do?

You: I can focus on the friends I already have that are important to me.

ICK: What if you still feel embarrassed after talking to that person?

You: I can remind myself of my list of things I like about myself and remind myself that one person does not decide for me who I really am.

ICK: What if that takes a while to believe and you still feel uncomfortable for some time?

You: I can do something I find enjoyable to help myself feel better and remember that "this too shall pass."

Follow the fear. Talk it through in your head and make a plan for what you would do if the worst-case scenario really did happen at some point. But remember, the worst-case scenario is the one the ICK will *always* choose to show you. And it can't be right 100 percent of the time. No one is.

Let's try one more example of following the fear. Let's say that you failed a quiz that's worth 5 percent of your grade, so now you are worried about failing the whole course. The tiny grain of truth that the ICK uses says that failing is an actual possibility in the realm of real life; people can and do sometimes fail courses. What if you do fail? What would you do? We have to change the "what if" to an "I can." The "what if" in this example is "What if I fail?" Now to make that into an "I can" statement, ask yourself these questions: *What could I do if I did fail? How would I handle it?* Here's a possible "I can" response: "I can talk to my instructor about what he thinks I didn't understand from the quiz. I can also get a tutor, and I can always take the course again over the summer if I have to."

Now what usually happens next is that the ICK tries again. It doesn't give up easily. So now there is a new fear. It shifts and becomes, "What if my parents yell at me for failing?" Well, what could you do if that happened? "I can prepare myself before talking to them about failing, and have a plan ready to show them how I'm going to make up the course and do better next time." That might help! But ICK keeps at it:

ICK: What if the course isn't offered in the summer?

You: I can look up courses at other schools and see if they will transfer the credit to my school.

ICK: What if that doesn't work?

You: I can take the course again the next semester it is offered.

As new fears keep popping up, keep following the fear. Keep answering the question raised by the fear. The more you are able to do this, the more confident you will feel that you can handle anything that comes your way. You will feel more secure in your ability to problem-solve when things go wrong. If you get stuck on one of the "what ifs," you can go to a friend or family member, or even a counselor, to try to get some other ideas. This takes some practice, but always remember: change "what if" to "I can" and keep following the fear. This is how you will keep your power—the power that the ICK is trying to take from you by making you feel that the worst will always happen and that there's nothing that you can do about it. You *can* do something about it! You just need to remind yourself of that and not let the ICK take you for a spin.

You're on Your Way to Win This Battle

So now we have a healthy understanding of the thought traps that the ICK uses to take us down. We are armed with new knowledge and a few approaches to fight some of the thought traps that the ICK uses, like changing "what if" to "I can." Game on! We know that the ICK thrives when you feel your worst. Thus, it's going to use these "weapons of mass self-destruction" to keep you at your lowest. When you're low, ICK is high, so that's what it wants. Not on your watch!

We have covered three steps to dealing with the ICK's negativity so far: step 1—change "I" to "you"; step 2—visualize the gremlin (instead of the disguise it was using before) and picture the mean words coming out of its mouth (and laugh!); and now we have step 3—catch the thought traps. Check! You're almost there. If you can get this far, you've almost won the battle. Steps 1 to 3 are really difficult, because the hardest part is calling the ICK out on its behavior and trusting yourself. Once you notice the approaches the ICK uses, it's easier to see the reality of things that the ICK tries to disguise.

Now we get to move on to step 4: tap into your True Inner Voice. This can be a pretty tricky step to do, depending on how persuasive your ICK is, so let's make sure we have the background info on what your True Inner Voice is all about. Read on!

13

Your True Inner Voice

Step 4: Tap into Your True Inner Voice

Once you start to squish the ICK back down to size, there is usually a bit of a void in your head—no one is left talking; it's like silence. This is because your True Inner Voice has been squashed down by the ICK for so long that it is barely there as a whisper. This means the next challenge is to find your True Inner Voice and to start to amplify it so the ICK doesn't think it can come back in and take over again.

How do you find your True Inner Voice? To start off, it sounds compassionate and caring. It sounds like a best friend would in your head. Trust me, your True Inner Voice wants to be your best friend—it is *you* after all. The ICK can trick you into thinking otherwise, but at the end of the day, your True Inner Voice is there to help you, support you, encourage you, and uplift you. Just like a best friend.

When we talk about a compassionate inner voice, many people, at first, think, *Isn't that wimpy? Or weak?* Nope, it isn't weak! Tapping into that compassionate inner voice actually makes you stronger over time. Being tough on yourself isn't all that it's cracked up to be, even though the ICK can make you think this is true. In fact, being tough on yourself can often leave you feeling a heck of a lot worse about yourself in the long run, even if it happens to coincide with getting some stuff done. Chances are (and there is some solid science out there to support this) that you actually would have done a lot better at things in the past if you weren't so hard on yourself (Mallinger 2009).

It can be difficult to believe this when you keep relating the pattern of being mean to yourself with a positive outcome. You think they are related, cause and effect—bullying yourself is the only way you get things done. Shifting away from this mean inner voice to being nice to yourself can make you worry that you will be less productive or less successful. But it just isn't true. So let's remember the shoe metaphor right now—the reason you feel hesitant about this and the reason it can be hard to believe this is because new things are going to feel weird. But in order to get to that positive end goal, you have to try those new things anyway. This is one of those times to try something new: being compassionate to yourself. Trying out this compassionate tone will help you uncover and develop your True Inner Voice. Let's check out two different scenarios to understand this idea a little bit more.

Scenario 1: The Big Game

Think of a sport you used to play or a hobby you have learned. I'm going to use basketball as an example, since I was on the team in sixth grade (go me!). You can sub in your own sport or go along with me for the ride using this basketball story.

So imagine this. You're at a basketball game, and a foul has just been called. This means you get two free-throw shots. This is where everyone else on the team lines up on either side of the key by the net and stares at you, expecting you to throw two flawless shots into the basket since no one is stopping you from making these shots here but you. You've got all the time in the world, essentially, to rock these free throws. Your coach watches from the sidelines. You've practiced these shots so many times, this should be easy. (Notice that tricky "should" that got in there?) As you line up for the shot, your coach yells, "Get your eye on that basket! Don't screw this up! Don't you dare miss that shot! If you miss that shot, you'll let your whole team down. This entire game rests on your shoulders! If you miss, everyone will remember you as the kid who sucked at basketball and ruined the whole game!"

Now, of course, your heart rate has gone up, and the pressure is on. You sweat a little. You feel the ball slide a little in your grip, so you quickly wipe off your palms on your gym shorts. Then you go to line up for the shot again. All the while, you can still hear your coach yelling.

You finally take the shot. The ball sails through the air, but then bounces off the rim. Damn! Your coach yells louder, "What do you think you're doing?! This is so embarrassing. Everyone is watching you! You represent the whole team! Don't screw this up! You have to redeem yourself. You don't want to be known as the kid who missed two easy shots, do you?" So you wipe your brow, pretend you aren't upset, and try again. The ball flies through the air, hits the backboard and rebounds right into the eagerly waiting hands of your opponent, who then pivots and dodges her way back to the other end of the court. You try to get back on track in the game, but you can still hear your coach yelling at you. The spring has decidedly gone out of your step.

Oh, my goodness. Sad, right?? Luckily for me, my sixth grade coach wasn't like this. Now let's try the scenario again with a different coach.

Scenario 2: Rewind, Try Again

Okay, same game, same setup. You're waiting at the top of the key to make your shot, and you hear your coach from the sidelines. You're a bit nervous because you can feel everyone's eyes on you. But then you hear, "Do your best! Don't worry about everyone watching. You can do this! Just do your best; that's all anyone can ask for!" You feel a little uplifted, and some of the pressure just eased. You know your coach will forgive you even if you miss the shots. You'll try your hardest, but you know that not everyone is perfect, and so does your coach. Your coach understands that it's a high pressure situation and that you're doing the best you can. You feel a little more confident to make the shot, knowing that your life isn't going to be over if you fail.

You line up and shoot the ball, watch it hit the backboard and then circle the rim a few times like it's about to twirl down into the basket, but then it pops itself out and lands on the floor. Darn! So close! You look over at your coach hoping not to see disappointment in her eyes. You don't. She cheers you on again: "So close! That's was almost it! Give it another try; you can do this! It's a lot of pressure, but don't worry about it. The game is bigger than just these two shots. Do your best!" You hear your coach's words and think, *Yeah, it's true, even if I miss these points, it's not like I don't have another chance in the game to make up for it!*

You stand tall and strong, line up and get ready to shoot, and the ball flies through the air. Swish! Nothing but net! The crowd goes wild! Awesome! You quickly pat yourself on the back, hear your coach cheering congratulations, and then get back into the game, feeling positive and strong, with a definite spring in your step.

Coach Yourself to "Good Stress"

If you guessed that the coach story was a metaphor for your True Inner Voice versus your ICK, you were right. Your ICK is like the coach from scenario 1. It is super tough on you. It bullies you and is mean to you, thinking that this is the only way to get you to perform. It blows things out of proportion and catastrophizes. It picks away at your self-esteem until you are unable to perform at your best. Then your self-esteem drops even lower.

In scenario 1, you also got to see the body's reaction to stress—the sweating, reduced concentration, and increased heart rate. When your ICK yells at you, you feel anxious. Your body responds to this by producing stress hormones like adrenaline. This causes your heart rate to go up. It makes your body sweat. It also slows your digestion, which can cause a nauseous feeling.

Don't worry; this is all adaptive for times when you really *should* be anxious, evolutionarily. For example, if you ever were to run into a bear in a forest and you needed to run away really fast, increasing your breathing gets more oxygen to your muscles. Sweating cools you down so you can run longer. The energy that is redirected away from your digestion heightens your ability to run faster. These are all evolutionarily adaptive responses for more "natural" threatening situations. However, in cases where you're just attempting a free-throw shot, too much of this isn't helpful. When the ICK lays on the stress at super high levels, the body responds in a way that reduces your ability to perform well. This bullying approach is not helpful.

What about in scenario 2? Well, that seemed to go a lot better. And while it's a nice story that I made up in this case, it's also not far from the truth. Science supports the fact that when you use positive self-talk and are nice to yourself, your ability to perform will actually increase (Hatzigeorgiadis, Zourbanos, Mpoumpaki, and Theodorakis 2009). By moderating the amount of stress you feel, your body stays in the "good zone" of stress. A smidge of stress can actually increase your performance, but too much puts you over the edge. A competitive situation will naturally cause a bit of anxiety or stress, so the job of the True Inner Voice is to moderate this through positive, compassionate self-talk that makes you feel supported and confident. Then you stay in the "good zone" of stress, and you are more likely to be successful. This works for sports situations, social encounters, presentations, and tasks big and small. It impacts every aspect of your life.

Now that you know what tone your True Inner Voice uses, and you can pick out the bullying voice of your ICK as well as what thought traps it uses, you can start to think about what your True Inner Voice would really be saying to you.

Step 5: Find More Realistic Replacement Thoughts

Your True Inner Voice sounds like a best friend would. It says to you the kinds of things that you say to your friends. It is far less reactive, emotional, and negative than your ICK, and it is fair to you at all times. It makes sure to look at all sides of a scenario. It doesn't use words like "always" or "never," and it doesn't ever call you names. It doesn't have the right answers all the time, but it makes sure not to jump to the negative answers instead when it isn't sure of all the details of a situation, like your ICK would. When unsure, instead of making you feel like the worst will happen, your True Inner Voice steps back from situations and helps you take a few deep breaths, then thinks things through to find answers and solutions and ideas, and it makes sure that you are always supported. It helps you feel confident, and it reminds you of why you are worthwhile. It uses words like "sometimes," "often," "maybe," and "possibly." It notices thought traps and then breaks them down into more realistic thoughts.

To help yourself connect your True Inner Voice with more realistic replacement thoughts, imagine a good friend, family member, mentor, or positive role model as the voice in your head. What would that person say to you? Now say that to yourself. Never berate yourself, but explain things to yourself nicely. Don't bully yourself, but converse with yourself with respect. Even try asking yourself, *If I were talking to my friend instead of myself, what would I say to that friend?* This is how you can start to find these more realistic replacement thoughts. For instance, perhaps your ICK says to you, "There you go, procrastinating again, you never get anything done on time, you can't do anything right." This is where you step back, realize that this sounds like a giant bully in your head, shrink it down to size, tap into how a friend might sound, and then balance out the thought. Notice that your ICK is overgeneralizing and using all-or-nothing thinking. Take out the word "never." Change the language so it's not so mean. In a situation like this, your True Inner Voice might say something like, "You probably have taken a long enough break. Maybe it would be a good idea to get started on homework now. I know sometimes you can get a bit distracted, so why don't we get started by getting out our books to get the ball rolling?" Your True Inner Voice turns this conversation into a helpful, realistic, and balanced discussion that helps you get things done in a much healthier and much more productive way, with your self-esteem intact.

Now that we've made our way through each of the five steps in more detail, let's bring everything together. First, we'll put the five steps all together in another example, and then, second, in your own personal movie scene so that you'll never forget how to defeat your greatest opponent. Bring on the Epic Battle of the ICK!

14

The Epic Battle of the ICK: Starring You

Conversations with Yourself

Every good movie has dialogue. In this Epic Battle of the ICK, the script is a conversation with yourself. Not the "maybe you should speak with a doctor about that condition, it may require medical attention" kind, but the kind we all actually have in our heads all the time, even though not everyone talks about it. These conversations with yourself are some of the most important ones you will have in your life, even more so than with friends, family, or even significant others. This is because, as mentioned earlier, you are the only person in your life who you will ever spend 100 percent of your time with. Thus, the way you talk to yourself in your head is one of the most impactful, important voices you will ever hear. Here is where we really keep building on step 4 ("tap into Your True Inner Voice") and step 5 ("find more realistic replacement thoughts").

Do you ever dread spending time alone? Do you shudder at the thought of doing tasks or activities by yourself? This could be an indication that your conversations with yourself aren't going too well, and that maybe your ICK is getting the upper hand. It's that same feeling you get when you don't want to hang out with the mean kid in class or the strict teacher who yells a lot. The voice inside your head is one that you can't escape, and it is exhausting to try. At one time or another, this happens to all of us. This means that we need to practice talking to ourselves in a way that makes us look forward to nights when we get to stay in and hang with ourselves. Party of one!

Let's try an example and work through all the steps here. We'll work with a common ICK phrase about dating, because the ICK likes to use this topic a lot to get at our overall self-esteem. Let's assume that voice in your head sounded like this: *No one will ever like me; it's obvious. If that girl I tried to talk to didn't want to date me, no one will ever want me.* Let's see what we can do with this little treasure from the ICK.

Step 1: Replace the "I" with "you." Now, instead, the ICK says to you in your head, *No one will ever like you; it's obvious. If that girl you tried to talk to didn't want to date you, no one will ever want you.* Hmm, okay, better—step 1 is complete. But, of course, we aren't done yet, because that's still not a very nice thing to say in our own head.

Step 2: Visualize the gremlin. Shrink the ICK down to size and see it for what it really is. Visualize the little gross green gremlin, add a funny voice and some over-the-top hand gestures. Imagine the gremlin saying that same sentence, instead of it coming from a more intimidating source in your head. Funnier now, isn't it! Less intimidating now that you can see this verbal attack isn't coming from your True Inner Voice after all.

Step 3: Catch the thought traps. Now we can step back and think for a second. Did the ICK just say, "Because that girl didn't want to date you, no one would ever want you?" Stop the ICK: that's the thought trap of overgeneralization! Nice try. You caught that pesky thought trap that the ICK tried to use!

Step 4: Tap into your True Inner Voice. Now let's picture that second coach. You know, the nice one, the supportive one, the one who can see things as being more realistic instead of pessimistic. Imagine a friend, loved one, or mentor and the tone of voice that he might use. Imagine his intentions as he speaks to you, wanting to lift you up and help you do well in your life.

Step 5: Find more realistic replacement thoughts. Now what would that True Inner Voice say to you? It would probably say something like, *Just because that person didn't want to date you doesn't mean that someone else won't. You're a good catch, and you just need to find the right person—someone who appreciates you for who you are. It's actually a good thing that girl was honest, because who wants to spend time with someone who doesn't actually like him? Not you! You want someone who will appreciate you for everything that you are. Now that you know she isn't interested, great. You can now spend your time continuing to look for someone who is going to be the right match for you. It sucks, and it hurts a bit, but it will be okay and you will feel better in a few days. You will find the right person; you just have to keep looking! You're too great of a person to be alone; it's just going to be a matter of time!* That certainly sounds more like your True Inner Voice!

And voilà, suddenly you don't feel so bad anymore. That was a much-needed reality check from your True Inner Voice.

Applying this approach can stop the world from crashing down on your head like the ICK wants it to, even when negative things happen in life.

Now here's a very important check-in for you to do: Did you think that the True Inner Voice's response was cheesy? Did you think it was fake and unrealistic? If so, it's not surprising. That's the ICK trying to talk you out of fighting back against it. You may be so used to the ICK's voice that your True Inner Voice sounds weird. And what did we learn about weird? It doesn't mean it is wrong. Just like those new shoes, you have to try it out and give it a chance, and eventually it will feel natural.

Cheat Sheet of Steps

You now officially have all the tools at your disposal to take the ICK out at the knees, and we took one practice round. Let's put it all together in a single, seamless epic battle:

Step 1: Change "I" to "you."

Step 2: Visualize the gremlin.

Step 3: Catch the thought traps.

Step 4: Tap into your True Inner Voice.

Step 5: Find more realistic replacement thoughts.

There is your cheat sheet of wisdom. Come back to this page whenever you need to. You can jot the steps down on a wallet-sized card and keep it with you, or type it on a note in your phone. Now let's finish off this scene to end our battle against the ICK. We've spent all this time learning about how to go through our steps; it's time to see how everything comes together on the big screen. It's movie time. This will make it easier to remember all the steps when your ICK is fighting back, full force! This movie scene, starring *you*, will pop into your mind, and you will be able to sail through the steps with lightning fast precision! Lights, camera, action!

Roll the Cameras

The lights come up. There you are, in the middle of a foggy battlefield. You know who you want to become and what you want to do with your life, but alas, there is an obstacle in your way. You face off in the battlefield of your mind, up against your most difficult opponent—the ICK. You turn to face it, readying yourself for battle. It towers above you, casting its shadow over you. You look up, up, and up, and there it stands—huge and intimidating and going wild! It is shouting things, gesturing, and using all your biggest fears against you. It is so frightening! You begin to cower in fear, hearing the tiny grain of truth that the ICK is wailing against you, but then you steel yourself, remembering your strength and vowing to tackle this ungodly beast.

What do you do? At first, you're unsure; you've never really faced off with your ICK before, and you don't know how this is going to turn out. Maybe you should just back away, like you usually do. But you say to yourself, *No!* You remember that you need to give it a try, even though it feels scary and uncomfortable. So you pull a massive sword of wisdom out of your sheath (yes, that's right—I just gave you a sword and sheath, and while we're at it, you've got some armor now, too!) and you hold it high above your head. You feel the strength from your sword transferring down into your arms, so you take a deep breath and mentally prepare to take your first swing.

As you hold your sword of wisdom (the wisdom of your five steps, of course), you stop, listen, and gauge your approach. You notice how the ICK uses your own voice against you. It keeps saying "I," disguising itself as your True Inner Voice. You see through this tactic, knowing the ICK is trying to trick you. You know what to do about this. You take the ICK's words and throw them right back, changing "I" to "you," and taking away some of its power for step 1. As you change "I" to "you," you feel your muscles strain as you heave the sword through the air, slicing forward as you take your first swing at your ICK: swoosh! You take a chunk off the side of the ICK, which falls through the air and fizzles into smoke as it hits the ground. The ICK quickly regroups and reforms itself so it is half of its original the size. It shakes off the damage and turns to face you again. You feel your confidence rise as you realize you do have some power over your opponent. You've completed the first step. You lift yourself up and prepare for round 2.

The ICK tries again. It keeps shouting at you, but now it has to use the word "you" instead of "I," because you and your sword of wisdom stripped it of this trick. But hark! Despite its efforts to continue to shout at you and make you retreat, without its trick of disguising itself as your True Inner Voice, you start to see right through it. You know how you can make it even less intimidating and see it for what it truly is. You know there's another disguise to be taken off. You wind up for another swing and swoosh! You take off another chunk of the ICK that falls to the ground and fizzles into smoke. The ICK re-forms to half its size again, and now you see it as it truly is: small and green and slimy. It looks like an ugly little gremlin—step 2 is complete! How funny it seems now, still shouting and flailing around, trying to make you feel bad about yourself! You throw your head back and laugh deeply, knowing you're only three steps away from defeating your enemy. Steps 1 and 2 were scary to try at first, but now that you've done them, you know you're ready for steps 3, 4, and 5!

You feel yourself standing a little taller and a little stronger when you start to look for those nasty little thought traps. You quickly and easily pick out a blatantly obvious example of overgeneralization, and even notice a tricky "should," one of the hardest thought traps to catch! These bounce right off your armor now that you recognize them! You are impervious to their effects, because you know how they work! You take a deep breath and begin to smile as you wind up to take another swing at those thought traps for step 3. Swoosh! You cut the gremlin down again, watching the smoke swirling up and around as the gremlin tries to reform itself. It is getting smaller and weaker by the moment.

The ICK, now no bigger than a mouse, shakes its fist up at you, still trying to bring you down with its words. You laugh, holding your stomach, reveling in your newfound power and freedom. Its voice is high and squeaky now, and it just sounds silly. It is much quieter; you can now barely hear it. You listen closely. You think you start to hear something else. Yes, yes, there it is! You begin to hear your True Inner Voice. It sounds like a good friend, and you find the source of that voice and turn up the volume. You found step 4! You hear your True Inner Voice supporting you, encouraging you, and cheering you on. It understands you and knows you're doing your best. You smile as you sheath your sword of wisdom, cross your arms, and focus on your True Inner Voice. It helps you see the situation as it really is. It reminds you of all the reasons you have to be confident and helps you find your realistic replacement thoughts for step 5. You are reminded why you like yourself, and why you're going to be okay. It reassures you that you can get through this and any situation that comes your way. As you feel yourself getting stronger, the ICK finally realizes that it has lost this battle, and it scampers away, tail between its legs. You smile knowingly; this will not be the last you see of the ICK, but you know you can defeat it when it rears its ugly head again. You are ready to take it on—any place, anytime.

End scene.

And the Crowd Goes Wild!

You've done it! You've really, truly done it! Okay, well, fictional movie-character-you has done it, but now you're on the road to success armed with this new information. These steps will help you figure out how to shut down the ICK once and for all, whenever it might appear. Now this will take some practice, of course. It may not always seem as easy as movie-character-you made it seem, but it will get easier with time.

Don't be too hard on yourself as you start to practice this, and forgive yourself if you don't get it right all the time. Just keep at it, and eventually it will start to seem like second nature, like practicing any skill in life! I believe in you. Seriously, if you've made it this far in reading this book, you're going to be just fine if you keep practicing. Many people put down a book like this one after a few pages, but not you. That means that you are determined to make this work. So you will! Personal yield theory (from part 1, chapter 3, where we talked about why you are who you are) dictates that once you know better, you can do better. You are arming yourself with knowledge (your handy sword of wisdom) so that next time you are faced with a situation where the ICK seems larger than life, you'll know what to do. You've changed your path in life simply by learning more. And the more you practice these things, the better you'll be in time. Go you!

We now have two more tricks to tackle that the ICK likes to use—using your body's natural reactions to lower your self-esteem through the thought trap of emotional reasoning, and then adding onto that with a big ol' negative label. The more we learn about each of these tricks that the ICK can get a hold of, the better we will be at defeating all of its sneaky maneuvers! Let's look first at labels.

15

Labels Are for Soup Cans

Body and Brain and Emotions, Oh My!

You now know that the ICK is something we all have. You also now know some of the tricks it plays. But most importantly, you now have a method to defeat it. You can probably look back at some really bad days you've had and recognize that your ICK was in full force at the time. The ICK often has the power to change your mood, confidence, and thought patterns. This can change what you say, do, think, or feel, usually for the worse. Thus, on some days, depending on how strong your ICK is, this probably makes a different version of yourself come to the forefront.

Hold up a second. What does that even mean—"a different version of yourself"? There are a few times now where I've talked about different versions of yourself—Past You, Present You, and Future You. We'll talk more about these versions of yourself as we keep working through the book. However, there are also daily versions of yourself. These are different pieces of yourself that come to the forefront at different times for different reasons. Some of these have to do with mood, which we'll talk about in the next section, and some are linked to your physiology.

You can probably now see that the ICK has likely played a big role in different daily versions of yourself depending on what that ICKy inner voice was saying to you at the time. It makes sense that other influences have an impact on who you may be at any given moment as well. Your physiology also plays a role. Hormones (which include stress hormones and sex hormones) and other chemicals in your brain called "neurotransmitters" are some of the other biggest influences. These neurotransmitters are chemicals in your brain that help deliver messages to other parts of your brain. Some of these fancy neurotransmitters are called serotonin and dopamine, and these are largely responsible for your mood: they are the "happy" chemicals in your brain. They get released during events in life like eating food, exercising, and being close with people you love.

Usually, all these different hormones and neurotransmitters get released in reaction to events. You run into a bear in the woods? Stress hormones help make you run faster, farther, and longer so that you can live to tell the tale. Hit puberty? Sex hormones get you ready to reproduce so your genes will be passed down from your DNA for future generations to adore. Hug someone you love? Dopamine and serotonin help you to feel happy and connected to people so that you can continue to live as a part of a community and be more likely to survive (think caveman times—without a clan, you probably weren't going to make it through winter alone). All of these hormones and neurotransmitters help to regulate your mood and create reactions in you that help you live a longer, better life. They all serve a purpose.

Colliding with the Modern World

So what does this mean? It means that some of your current reactions and emotions are dictated by past evolutionary events that have connections to your physiology—and are not really linked to your personality or skill set at all! Some of these reactions, like stress for instance, can make you think you're not good at something because your body goes into freak-out mode. However, this is really just an example of our modern world colliding with past evolutionary influences. For instance, just because an anxiety response makes it possible for you to outrun a bear doesn't mean that it helps you when you have that in-class presentation you have to do. When your stress hormones get released in response to a high-pressure situation, and your body reacts in a way that is supposed to help it run longer, farther, and faster, this doesn't always mean that it is a helpful response to the task in the present. A stress response that makes you shake the cue cards right out of your hands and breathe at five times the normal rate when you're trying to talk doesn't seem like the best physiological reaction for the modern world. This is because the anxiety response did not evolve for this modern situation—it evolved for running away from bears.

Because of the differences between the responses we needed in caveman times and what we need now, these types of physiological responses can sometimes be a bit confusing. Let's look further at public speaking, for example. If you're at the front of a classroom of people about to give a speech and your entire body starts sweating and you feel like you need to throw up, you might be sincerely convinced that you are less than capable of this task. But this is just a different version of yourself

(Scared You) in response to an event, and in this case, this version of yourself is linked to a physiological reaction.

And watch out, because this is where the ICK will try to trick you into some emotional reasoning (remember that thought trap) so you think that this is truly a permanent shortcoming of your overall personality. You may forget to stop and check in on what this version of yourself is up to. This check-in can be done by literally talking to yourself inside your head, and saying, *Hey there, Self, whatcha doin'? Why are you freaking out?* Remind yourself that there is no actual bear chasing you in this situation. Take a bit of time to think about your strengths and your resilience even in a state of anxiety, and separate yourself from the physiological reactions taking place. You can function even when your body experiences anxiety if you take some deep, calm breaths, slow your thoughts down by taking one thought at a time, and then check in with your "what ifs," and use your "I can"s. Then make sure you challenge any thought traps you find (step 3), tap into your True Inner Voice (step 4), and find more realistic replacement thoughts (step 5).

Just Say No to Negative Labels

In the scenario above, your body has gone into "being scared" mode, so you automatically believe there is truly something to fear. This is an ICKy thought trap of emotional reasoning: because you are reacting with fear, there must truly *be* something to fear. You then might think that you really do suck at public speaking, and it is truly terrifying. If you don't check in with what this version of yourself is doing and why this is happening, you might fall into the trap of layering this logic

109

onto your identity of yourself for all time. If you label yourself as "weak" or "inept" or "terrible at public speaking," or whatever term you come up with at the time because your in-class presentation went pretty badly, that isn't really a fair assessment! That situation only means that, at that particular point in life, in front of a group of people, your body went into a stress response. This is physiological, but it can actually be changed with time, practice, persistence, and positive internal dialogue. It is not a permanent condition; it is a version of yourself, on that day, at that time, in that situation.

Understanding these facets of yourself and the different pressures that you may be under at various times (as well as some of the physiology behind it) can help you separate yourself from a negative feeling or bodily reaction. It can keep your ICK from labeling you with a permanent personality flaw.

When you label yourself, you actually stifle your ability for future growth because you see that label as permanent and unchanging. Permanent negative labels should be avoided at all costs. Self-awareness—like knowing that you can work on your presentation skills because you have lots of room to improve—is great, but labeling yourself as "inept" will only hinder your ability to grow. This is because we tend to act in ways that keep in line with our labels and our understanding of ourselves.

We do this to avoid something called *cognitive dissonance* (the mental state of discomfort when our personally held beliefs don't match up with our behaviors or experiences). In order to avoid the discomfort of cognitive dissonance, we work very hard to prove our already held beliefs to be true. And when this is in the form of a permanent label, our brains want to believe that what we already know is true, so we don't want to change those beliefs. We don't like being proven wrong, even by ourselves. Thus, if the labels we have for ourselves are negative or limiting, we can become trapped in a cycle of proving ourselves right even when it's not in our best interest.

The Cycle Ends Here

Let's look at an example to see how cognitive dissonance keeps your self-esteem low and your ability to perform hindered when you use negative labels. In the example above, if you had labeled yourself as "bad at public speaking" due to your physiological fear response, this could actually cause you to believe that you are bad at public speaking for all time. Then, with this label, you would continue to confirm this belief in order to avoid the discomfort of cognitive dissonance. That discomfort would be caused by having to change your understanding of yourself, which our brains avoid doing because it takes energy. So to confirm this negative label, you would likely then avoid public speaking and become very anxious if you did have to speak in public. By avoiding the task, you would hinder your ability to grow and become better at public speaking because you would never get to practice. By getting anxious because of the negative label (since no one gets excited about having to do something that they think they are terrible at), you would hinder your ability to perform further because you have now amplified your anxiety response instead of reducing it, and you may actually perform worse in the future. These actions and outcomes confirm the label. This lets you stay mentally comfortable—but it limits your growth and development of your skills and abilities. And then the label sticks.

Acknowledging that physiological influences are separate from your personality and also avoiding negative labels really does work. To bring this idea home, I've got a little story to share. I can attest to it! I've hit you with a lot of stories about fictional people so far, so let me tell you a real story about me this time. It's kind of entertaining, I think.

I remember having to give a presentation in my ninth grade science class, and I was having a strong physiological anxiety reaction. This caused my mouth and throat to become very dry and very tense, making it difficult to speak and breathe. Because of this, I literally sounded like I was going to cry for the whole ten-minute speech; anxiety was hitting me full force. Now I'm sure this was probably very embarrassing, but I didn't really get too concerned. I gave the speech anyway. I got through it. I didn't label myself as a failure and run out of the room, never to return to public speaking again. Why not? Because I knew that this was just something that was happening to me because I was nervous. So when I was done, and my friends asked me what the heck that was all about, I just shrugged and said that my body does weird things when I have to present, but I still have to present anyway so that's what you get. Then we laughed about it and it was fine. I avoided the negative label of "bad public speaker" because I knew that the physiological response was completely normal, and that it was the cause of my difficulties—not something that couldn't be overcome at some point.

My physiology didn't dictate my skill. I still had a good presentation and a lot of good things to say. Anxiety was just something happening to me. It wasn't the real me. I knew what I was talking about and I knew I wanted to tell people about it, but I realized that it was going to take some time practicing in public for the anxiety to dissipate. I knew that, in time, I could eventually get better at public speaking if I practiced more, even though it was uncomfortable.

So what happened because I was able to avoid this permanent negative label? I ended up going into teaching for a time, a profession where I essentially presented to people every single day. Then, as I got into teaching more and more frequently in front of more and more students, after a while, the stress response I used to experience simply went away. My body learned there was nothing to fear as I got continued exposure to public speaking. If I had attached a label of "bad public speaker" to myself, I doubt I would have gone into teaching at all. So there you have it; make sure you avoid those pesky negative labels!

To sum up: does it mean you are weak or inept if you get nervous in front of large groups? Nope. You're just human, and all you have to do is work on your body's response to fear. This can be done with practice and exposure, and by talking yourself through the realities of the situation. Be careful that your ICK doesn't apply negative labels to your True Self based on some smaller facets of your physiology that aren't permanent traits. This applies to lots of different situations, temporary weaknesses, or less-than-ideal responses. It can be a physiological response that you get when you do homework, ask someone on a date, try something new, meet new people, or play a sport. Keep those negative labels away and allow yourself to be the most awesome version of you that you can be, even if it takes some practice! As we learned earlier, even if it feels weird, or even if something makes you anxious, it is normal and it will get better with time and exposure, so let yourself grow past the tough parts.

One Last Secret: Labels That Work

There is one more trick that I will share, which is that there is one type of label that can work in your favor. This is any positive, helpful label about yourself. Remember how we learned about cognitive dissonance and that we don't like to be proven wrong if we already believe something? Well, if you label yourself as something positive—friendly, outgoing, talented, and so on—this can work in your favor because you will work very hard to reaffirm that belief about yourself. That reaffirmation will allow those traits and skills to flourish and continue to develop. As we learned, we want to prove ourselves right. If we believe we are skilled at something, this will keep us trying to fulfill that belief and live up to our positive labels. Do this one! Use all the positive labels that you like. Go nuts! But if you stumble across a negative label, just say no and stop the cycle.

Now that you know how to handle the thought trap of emotional reasoning, and you have learned the importance of avoiding negative labels—and using positive ones!—it's time to delve into emotional reasoning one step further. We're going to talk about how to make sense of how you feel in various situations, on various days, and in various moods. This will help you outsmart that ICK regardless of the emotions you may feel at any given time.

16

Daily Facets of You: You're a Prism

Getting to Know All Your Facets

There are versions of yourself that are going to be angry, sad, anxious, bored, happy, and so on. Getting to know all these different facets of yourself is important—there are so many yous to get to know! There's Happy You, Sad You, Angry You, Jealous You, Nervous You, Excited You, and the list goes on! It's important to learn how you think and react as each of these versions of yourself. For instance, when you are Happy You, you're going to think and react differently to things than when you are Angry You. You could be faced with the exact same situation, but depending on which version of yourself you are currently experiencing, you may react differently in each case.

You know when you shine a light through a prism, and depending on how you turn it, the light comes out differently on the other side? That's you! Each flat part of a prism is called a facet, and depending on which facet might be facing toward the light source, the light beam gets angled out the other side differently and can create different shapes, colors, and rainbows, all from the exact same light source. This is just the same way that we interact with our world. We have different facets, or faces, of ourselves, which are based on our emotions. Whichever version of ourselves is "facing the light" can completely change how we interact with that situation, and this can shift and change the outcome.

It makes sense to check in with yourself as to which version of yourself you are at all times so that you know how you might be interacting with a situation—and reflecting your metaphorical light! The goal is to get to know all your facets, and then to understand how, together, all these facets make up the whole prism of you. Once you understand yourself as a whole—your Whole Prism Self—then you can help yourself think, react, and speak so that you represent *all* of yourself at *all* times—or at least as best you can! This is especially important in situations where one facet might make a decision that doesn't jibe with the rest of your goals of your Whole Prism Self.

Have you ever seen someone make a hasty decision when really angry or upset, just to realize later that it wasn't what she really wanted overall? That person reacted as only a facet of herself instead of as her Whole Prism Self. She only reacted with part of herself instead of how she maybe wished she would have acted if she had been more balanced. How about when someone says something when she's really sad that she regrets saying once she's feeling better? Again, she spoke as a facet of herself, not as her Whole Prism Self. This isn't what we want for you.

The goal for you is to be able to see and understand your moods, emotions, and reactions when you are different versions of yourself (Sad You, Angry You, Scared You) and for you to be able to learn and understand your patterns. Then you can try to react in a way that will make you happy when you are your Whole Prism Self again.

Let's check out an example. For instance, if you experience an angry version of yourself, make sure you notice it and check in on it, and say something to yourself like, *Hey, this is Angry Me. I know that when I am Angry Me, I tend to blow things a bit out of proportion. I realize I'm doing this right now, so it might help to take a step back until I calm down. Once I get a bit calmer, I'm going to look at this problem again and see if I'm still as upset about it later on. If I am, I can do something about it. If not, maybe I can move on from it.*

Without doing this, you can fall into the trap of believing that Angry You is completely right in that moment—thought trap: emotional reasoning! You can ruin friendships or relationships, or make decisions that don't take your Whole Prism Self into consideration. When you slip into one small facet of yourself (Angry You, Sad You, Scared You, and so on), don't forget the bits of yourself that fell into the background. They're all still there, and you wouldn't want just one part of you to get to speak for the whole package.

When you start to feel very strong emotions, stop yourself for a moment. Take a breath. Take another. Then take a moment to figure out which version of yourself you are feeling. Say it to yourself. Say *I am Angry Me right now.* Remind yourself what your tendencies are when you are Angry You. Do you yell when you don't mean to? Do you push people away and regret it later? Tap into that facet and remind yourself what your Whole Prism Self would want you to do when your emotions are less intense. Give yourself time to pull all of your facets together before you make any big decisions. When possible, make sure you're back to your Whole Prism Self before you have any important conversations, and tell the people that are involved in the situation with you what you are trying to do. Tell them you need some space to cool off or think, and that you'd like to talk later once you've had some time to do this. Then come back to the issue when you are able to access your Whole Prism Self. Future You will be grateful that you did.

Past, Present, and Future Versions of You

Future You—how many versions of you *are* there? Well, funny you should ask—that's what this section is about. So what is Future You? It's the version of you that is disappointed when it realizes you watched TV all night instead of doing your homework. It's the one that feels super guilty that you yelled at your significant other over something small and inconsequential. It's the one that wishes that you had just stopped to talk to that person you thought was interesting, even though you were scared at the time. Future You is trying to tell you something, if you'll listen.

When you get into situations where you have a choice—the easy way where you do what feels best in the moment, or the hard way where you do something you don't want to do in the moment for the sake of the future—think about what the outcome was the last time something similar happened. What did you wish you had done last time when Future You reflected on the choices that Past You made? These types of decisions work best when you get all versions of yourself on the same page (Past, Present, and Future You all working together). This is tricky to do because Present You is usually going to want to take the easy route, but Future You always wishes you did things in your long-term best interests. How do you get Future You to help out Present You? Here's my favorite example for myself, in getting Present Me to think about Future Me, and having everyone work together.

I am not great in the mornings. I tend to always run two or three minutes late (or more) and when I was younger, this caused me a lot of grief. I would miss the bus, I would annoy my parents, and I would forget things because I was rushing at the last minute. So I started listening to Future Me. Future Me was always disappointed in Past Me—disappointed that I didn't just get things done five minutes earlier. After all, what's five minutes, really?? So Present Me decided she would try to help out and she set her clocks all five minutes faster. This helped a lot.

But then there were other things, like preparing lunches for the day. The night before, when I knew I should probably make my lunch, Present Me would always say, "Oh, I'll just make lunch in the morning." So I would put it off, even though I had time that evening to do it, because the couch was just so much more inviting in the moment. Now would that lunch ever get done in the morning, knowing that Present Me sucks in the mornings? Nope! Then Future Me would always be pissed that I didn't just do it when I had the time the night before, because I was always rushed in the mornings. So I started listening to Future Me. I would put something together for lunch before bed, even if it was just a can of soup, a can opener, and a bowl. We (Present Me and Future Me, that is) talked it through by compromising on an easy lunch solution, and Present Me got on board. In having this conversation with myself the night before, even if I was exhausted, Present Me realized that Future Me was going to be so grateful that I'd gotten a lunch together. It's kind of like doing a favor for a friend and getting thanked the next day. Now every morning when I'm on time and have a lunch, I thank Past Me. Good work, I say! And I really mean it, too, because I remember the night before was awful and I was tired, and I didn't want to do it, but I did it anyway—just for me! Thanks, me! And then we—Past, Present, and Future Me—have a mini party in my head for being able to do things as a team.

All the Versions of You on One Team

Seems a bit weird, perhaps, to talk to yourself in the past, present, and future in your head, but what a difference it can make. Not only do you have different versions of yourself on an emotional scale (Sad You, Angry You, Frustrated You, Happy You) and a physiological scale (Scared You, Tired You, Anxious You), you also have different versions of yourself in the past, present, and future. The things you do for yourself today as Present You, even if it's hard, will help Future You more than you might know. So keep track of the times when Present You looks back on Past You and is really disappointed.

This is all just about learning how to set yourself up for success. This is learning from your past and looking into what you think you'd like to do differently next time—how you could set yourself up better in the future. Add into the mix an understanding of different facets of yourself—physiologically, emotionally, and situationally—and you've cracked the code to success.

Let's look at an example of how all the versions of yourself can learn to work together in the context of personal yield theory. Perhaps in the past you started a fight with a partner or friend when you reacted in the moment as Frustrated You. It made sense for who you were at the time and the situation in the moment; you were doing the best you could at the time. You did not know what you know now, after having read this far in this book. However, now you can look back and learn from that encounter for the sake of Future You. Future You realized you didn't actually like that outcome and would like to do things differently next time so that this kind of thing doesn't happen again. That means it is time to reflect back, learn, and problem-solve for the future. You can ask yourself some questions like these:

What could I do differently in the future so that the same thing doesn't happen again?

What warning signs in myself should I look for to stop Frustrated Me from reacting the same way next time?

How can I have a talk with my partner or friend before the next fight to help her recognize when I'm losing my temper so she can help give me space?

What can I say to myself in my head to try to slow myself down next time?

Is my ICK at work here?

How can I tackle what my ICK is putting in my head?

How can I get my positive second coach, my True Inner Voice, on board to talk me through those moments in the future?

How can I take a couple of deep breaths next time to slow myself down?

These are the types of things you can think about next time to help out Future You. And then all the versions of you are all working together as you move forward in life.

The Self-Time Continuum

Past You, Present You, and Future You create what I call a "self-time continuum." (Get it? Like space-time continuum?) This refers to the connection among all three versions of ourselves. It refers to the trap we can often fall into of believing that our Past Self knew more than it actually did. It also refers to the trap of believing that our Future Self will be way better or different than it actually is. The key to this theory is to recognize that our Present Self is essentially the same person as both our Past and Future versions, just separated by a few days, weeks, months, or years. To project drastically different people onto these ends of the continuum will skew the way you live in the present.

To look at this continuum, let's go back in time to see how we might have projected things inaccurately on our own personal self-time continuum. Do you remember when you were eight years old, and you thought of who you were going to be when you were in high school? How far off were you? Did you imagine yourself doing things that didn't really fit your personality? If this is too far back to remember, think of a more recent example. Think of your age right now, and the last time you thought about what you would be doing at this age. Did you overproject? This is an example of projecting into the future on a different continuum than the one you are on.

My personal example is—and I remember this vividly—when I was in kindergarten at age five, I wanted to be a veterinarian when I grew up. I remember writing in my journal for school on that giant faded yellow paper pad with the giant fat red pencil. I wrote that by the time I was ten years old, I would be volunteering at a vet's office. I remember thinking, *Man, I am going to be ten! That is double my age! People who are ten are so old! I will have so much done by then!* But I clearly didn't understand this self-time continuum, and didn't realize how long it sometimes takes to learn things in life. I projected a far more advanced ten-year-old version onto my Future Self than was actually possible. I remember turning ten years old and thinking back to my predictions and how sad it was that I wasn't as far along as I thought I would be (but also how unreasonable my expectations had been).

But the key point of that story is that I wouldn't have felt sad had I known better how to project ahead along the self-time continuum. Knowing your own scale of time and change is important to being able to project ahead in a way that isn't going to leave you feeling guilty. When you tell yourself you'll be married with kids and a house by age twenty-eight, you may not realize that this doesn't fit with your own scale of growth and change. And the problem doesn't come from "not being good enough" to meet those goals—the problem comes from making goals that slide off the continuum. No one's continuum is "wrong"; it just *is*. We are each on our own journey in this life, and the rate at which we change and grow is right for each of us—at our own pace, in our own life, in our own circumstances.

That example can help us to remember not to commit ourselves to a goal or a life too far off in the future. Having some ideas of where you might go or where you might end up can be helpful, but it's also helpful to remember that your journey can change drastically in a large amount of time.

The self-time continuum is even more potent in short-term examples. These can be a bit more obvious to catch. A shorter-term example of the self-time continuum is one I get from a lot of the students I work with. They imagine a very different version of themselves as their Future Self, regarding all the homework they will do "later." They jump off of their own self-time continuum and imagine their Future Selves as super productive, very fast workers, and totally organized, which is not a realistic portrayal of how they actually work right now. With this idea that they will be a very different person in the very near future, they then leave things until later, thinking they will have lots of time because they will be so productive later on. Then, when the future arrives, they feel overwhelmed and disappointed when they can't work as fast as they thought they would, or they weren't as organized as they hoped they would be. In the self-time continuum, this means that they projected a false Future Self forward—one they wished they could be in the future, but one that they didn't give themselves a realistic time frame to achieve. They wanted all their procrastination problems to disappear in a few days, and didn't stop to remind themselves of their relationship with their Present Self.

Think about it. In just a few days or weeks, your Present Self will *be* your Future Self. Your Present Self and your Future Self are essentially the same people when they are only separated by a few days or weeks. So when you plan ahead, think of what is realistic for your Present Self. If you know that today, as your Present Self, you like to take long breaks when you do homework, don't project onto your Future Self that you will be able to work nonstop for five hours. Develop a plan that makes sense for who your Present Self is—a plan that has lots of breaks built in, and gives you enough time to work as you know you actually *do* work, not as you might like to work. You can always develop your skills over time, but this is a continuum of change that takes time, practice, and reflection to achieve—so keep your relationship with your Past You, Present You, and Future You realistic.

With this new understanding of your Whole Prism Self, all your different facets, the importance on reflecting for Past, Present, and Future You, and keeping your goals and your timeline reasonable on your own self-time continuum, you have even more tools to keep your ICK where it belongs. When your ICK tries to use these things against you through negative emotional reasoning and mismanaged expectations, and then when it tries to layer on the guilt and shame when it sets you up for failure, you can now fight back. Use this information to fight back when you go through step 5 of fighting back against the ICK—finding more realistic replacement thoughts. This can keep everything in perspective and remind you that you *can* do this, you *are* doing a good job in life, and you *will* be okay. Let's look at this idea a bit further.

17

The 80–20 Rule

You Can Do This

In part 2, you have read all about topics including who you are, ways to beat the ICK, thought traps, the tiny grain of truth, your true inner voice, labels, facets of yourself, your Whole Prism Self, and your self-time continuum. I hope that you can see a pattern starting to develop. Let's explore that a little more.

So far we have seen several examples showing us that many different things in life might happen, and that there are many possible outcomes and ways to react. We have also seen that there are many different ways to think about things that happen to us in our life. The most important thing that we have seen here is that what we think and how we react can truly dictate what the outcome will be for us. To be clear—life will throw all sorts of things at you. You can't always control those things. But what you do with those situations *is* up to you. You can't always control what comes your way, but you can control how you react. This gives us the 80–20 "rule":

**Life is 20 percent what happens to you,
and 80 percent how you react.**

That means that the 80 percent is much more important than the 20 percent—your reaction has more power than the situation in the grand scheme of life: the 80–20 rule. You can't always control what happens to you or what other people say or do. But you can choose to dwell on things or to stay stuck if things aren't going your way. You can let your ICK take over and not to fight back. You can let life go on without self-reflecting or without learning how to do better in the future. You wouldn't be the first person to fall into this trap.

OR…

Now that you know more, now that you have empowered yourself, now that you have learned your strengths and gotten to know the different facets of yourself, *you can change your future*. You can choose how you react. You can give yourself space and time to think and reflect. You can expose your ICK for what it truly is, and you can fight back and keep your self-esteem rockin'. You can remind yourself that even when things get tough, you can overcome them. You have the power. The cards are in your hands. You can do this!

Present You Is Off to the Races!

Take the momentum of what you have just learned, and plug it into the 80–20 Rule. You won't always have everything work out in life. At least 20 percent of it is simply out of your hands. But you can work out how you react and what your next steps are.

This is the 80 percent—how you react. Now that you have so many tools at your fingertips, you are really off to the races. You have your set of tools to tackle the ICK. You have the awareness of different facets and versions of yourself. You have ways to remember how to give your True Self a chance to speak or react as your Whole Prism Self instead of letting different facets react in the moment. You have a way to get Past You, Present You, and Future You all on the same team, and a way to remember how to set realistic expectations for yourself. Once you're working as a whole in each of these ways, your relationship with yourself will get better and better, and that will help you to like yourself—forever. You're so on your way to liking yourself now that we'll even move on to the last part of the book: The Future!

part 3

the future

18

Who Do You Want to Be?

Taking Your Next Steps

Now we are on to the future. This means you've looked through your past and accepted the place you are in now. You've reflected on your present and the various versions of yourself. You've even started to plow through the roadblocks to change. Now it's about deciding where to go next. You are feeling more confident in your ability to conquer your ICK when it gets you down, so your confidence is up and you want to continue to grow. You are starting to like yourself—flaws and all—and you are regaining control of your present. So now is the time to strengthen your relationship with yourself. And this means not accidentally hurting your relationship with yourself by holding yourself back from who you want to be, who you could be, or who you are meant to be. The more you know yourself, and the more you allow yourself to take chances and to do things you've always wanted to do, the stronger your relationship with yourself becomes. You are in this adventure called life with yourself—it's time to figure out where you want to go next now that you have a supportive True Inner Voice to help you out.

It's time to figure yourself out and break down any last remaining barriers holding you back from fully realizing the strength of the relationship that you can have with yourself. In this chapter, we'll look at how to do this, what choices to make, and also some good ways to practice new skills and to expand different parts of your current personality. Yay! Excitement!

Deciding for Yourself Who You Want to Be

Who do you want to be? This can be a tricky question, because there isn't one "right answer." And there are some reasons that the topic of "who you want to be" isn't easy to figure out.

One of these reasons is that, growing up, we always looked for confirmation from others—parents and friends, teachers and peers—that what we were doing was right, and we usually tried to do what was expected of us. We tended to believe them when they told us their opinion because we didn't know any better yet. We were young. We were learning about the world at this stage, and someone else always had more knowledge than we did. We deferred to others.

But at some point, we learn—and I mean truly *learn*, not just as a fact, but on an emotional level—that opinions can differ, and that's okay. We learn that, even though for a long time as a child we may have conformed to others' ideas, we finally see that there are indeed many different "right answers" out there. If you've already made this leap, good work! But read on; often there's still more work to be done on this journey, no matter how old you are. It may seem simple, but knowing something to be true and applying it in daily practice are two very different concepts.

After we truly understand this fact on an emotional level, we then start seeing the world in grays instead of in blacks and whites. It is at this point that we are at both a crossroad and a turning point. It's a crossroad because you can decide (or not) to take responsibility for making your own choices in life rather than just listening to adults because they are older. It is also a turning point because, whether you decide to take responsibility for your own choices or not, your life still changes, since you are becoming "older" and others recognize that. A nondecision is still a decision, and at some point, your life changes whether or not you choose to take on the responsibility of deciding for yourself. But here, in this book, I recommend embracing that decision to take responsibility for making your own choices in life, even though it can be scary. It strengthens your relationship with yourself to listen to your own True Inner Voice. When we finally become "old enough" that we realize things aren't simply wrong or right, but that there are many ways to look at things, we have the choice to listen to ourselves, or to everyone else, or some combination of the two. We see that all people have their grays, and that even older people with all of their "experience" still make decisions that could be considered "right" or "wrong," depending on how you look at the situation. This is when one's True Inner Voice starts to question if it, too, might be "right" even when someone else has a different opinion.

Here's the catch in making this transition—we have never been the expert before in life, so how do we make the shift from deferring to others to trusting ourselves with our own thoughts and decisions? How do we stand by our own opinions, knowing that we may be "right" but that someone else might *also* be "right," even though we think completely different things? And the hardest part is this—how do we finally feel okay about that when it happens? This is all new territory.

Now is the time to see that you can and you should move into a sense of confidence that your own opinion is *just as worthy* of consideration as that of your friends, peers, teachers, and parents. Why wouldn't it be? All of those people are just making their best guess in life—the same as you are. They're just people, too. It's time to decide that your voice, your opinion, and your ideas are just as valuable, worthwhile, and meaningful as everyone else's around you. Let's say that again. Your ideas are just as valuable, worthwhile, and meaningful as everyone else's around you!

It's All About You

In the end, it's all about you. It's your life, after all! Every day is an opportunity to continue to build yourself into who you want to be. According to personal yield theory, at any moment you may be faced with a decision, a dilemma, a problem, or an opportunity, and your ability to respond is based on who you have created yourself to be and the knowledge that you have built within yourself at that time.

You are the outline of a person from the day you are born, and each day thereafter you can paint in the picture. You can fill in your outline with skills, knowledge, experiences, and relationships, and you are always adding to this picture. You may sometimes find you are missing shades, colors, or images as you paint, but the beauty is that you can continue to add to this picture no matter how old you are. You can paint over old parts of yourself, knowing that traces of the image will remain, but that you can always create a new picture, image, and vision.

So it's time to start painting! It's time to start adding to the picture to create the version of yourself that you've always wanted to be. But here's the trick: this section will be a bit of a balancing act. It will be about pushing yourself, but also listening to yourself along the way. You want to unlock the parts of yourself that may be withdrawn or underdeveloped due to fear or lack of confidence, but you don't want to force yourself to be someone that you truly aren't. We're all unique, and this section of the book is about painting in your picture to find the best version of your True Self.

Finding Yourself Versus Creating Yourself

I was going to put this section in after I gave you all the steps to create your True Self, but then I got worried you'd get all excited, try all the steps, and then wouldn't get to this section for a while, so I put this section first. This is here to help you remember that while you go through the steps to creating yourself, the end goal is all about the balance of finding yourself versus creating yourself. This journey is about allowing yourself to become who you want to become (creating), while being open to learning from yourself as you go (finding). Who you *think* you want to be may not be who you *want* to be at the end of the day. I am sure you've probably seen at least one TV show or movie about a character that worked her whole life for "that thing"—be it medical school, a certain job, a certain relationship, or something else—but once she got there, realized that it wasn't actually for her. This is what we are talking about. You may have some ideas about who you want to *create* yourself to be, but remember to listen to yourself as you go to see if it actually makes you happy once you are there and if you find your True Self in the process.

As you look at creating the version of yourself you've always wanted to be, you'll realize that there are also some things that you actually want to keep the same, even if you didn't think so originally. This is not a bad thing! You should keep an eye on both finding yourself *and* creating yourself as you move forward through this section. So how do we look out for both?

To create the version of yourself that you would like to be while also finding your True Self, you have to do three things: (1) decide who you'd like to be, (2) try being that person (and make sure you give it enough time because new things often feel weird at first), and finally (3), once you've given being the person that you "want to be" a real solid shot, step back and reflect on that for a bit. Did it feel better just to try it out—like you're energized or like you've finally been released from a cage? If so, then you've probably found your True Self. And guess what?! You're lucky because it happened to correspond with the person that you thought you'd like to be. Don't worry, more detailed directions as to how to do all these steps will follow!

Now, what if you reflected back in that third step and it actually felt worse to be that "new" person, even though you gave it some time? What if you found it took way more energy and you were tired all the time, or what if you felt phony, beyond the feeling of it simply just being new and different? If it felt worse, it was probably not your True Self.

If it felt worse, now you need to reflect on why it was important to you to be that way in the first place. Why did you want that to be the "new you?" Was it something that someone else—for example, your family, friends, society, or culture—told you to be? Was it something that "people say" is a really good thing to be? People, society, or culture might not always know what's best for you. It may just not be right for you, and that's okay. In fact, that's great! Figuring out who we truly are is one of the biggest challenges most of us face in our lives. People can spend years questioning this without knowing how to find out for sure. Well, here's how! Take the above into account, and then read on, my friend. In this way, you will begin to discover your True Self while also creating the version of yourself that you've always wanted to be.

An Experiment in Finding Yourself

Let's look at Sally's story to look further at this concept of finding yourself versus creating yourself. When Sally thought about what she wanted to explore about herself, especially where she wanted to change and grow, she decided that she would like to be more outgoing to see if she was more extroverted than she thought she was. She thought back to some parties she had been to where she didn't really get to know anyone. She felt like she didn't have much fun because she mostly stayed in the corner of the room with the one or two people she already knew. She looked back at those times and remembered feeling really disappointed in herself and in the outcome of those parties, and she had the feeling that she'd missed some opportunities there. So Sally decided to take action after reading this book. Now, it may seem that there are a lot of steps in Sally's story, but don't worry. We will break the story down afterward and look at everything in detail so you can try the same approach that Sally used!

Begin scene.

Sally is on a mission to like herself, and so she decides she wants to try being more outgoing, to see if she maybe is more of an extrovert than she thought she was. She's creating the version of herself that she's always wanted, and feels that her shy past needs to take a backseat to the future version of herself that she's always wanted to be. So, she talks herself up, channels the energy of her outgoing role models, puts on her "fake it till you make it" approach (knowing that no one else knows who she is but her), and steps out into a few new situations being "outgoing Sally." She joins a new club or two and tests out "Sally 2.0," and plays this character for a few weeks with the new people she meets.

Sally pulls off this outgoing role pretty well. While a bit shaky at first, she steps out of her comfort zone and pushes her boundaries, and finds people respond to her well. Sally enjoys the feedback, but discovers that, at the end of her Sally 2.0 days, she is completely exhausted. Sally's body is trying to tell her something. She enjoys making new friends and being a lot more social, but the extent to which she has to talk and be social is draining, and she sincerely can't imagine doing this every day of her life. It's kind of fun once a week to try this out, but her whole life? That doesn't sound so good to her. Even if this is what she "thought" she wanted, or who she was "supposed" to be, Sally decides that this change is not something that is right for her. But she has learned some new skills from her venture into being Sally 2.0, which will help her in other areas of her life. She decides that she does like being a bit more outgoing, and she can make more friends in less busy settings where she has time to talk to people one on one. By recognizing the settings in which she finds it possible to make friends more comfortably, she balances her goal of making more friends with an approach that is more "naturally" her. She realizes she doesn't have to be the life of the party, but she can still be more outgoing while honoring her true introvert nature. She realizes that her introverted personality wasn't actually "getting in the way" of her True Self—it was her True Self, and that's okay! Now she can live her life as Sally the introvert, no longer having to feel ashamed that she was never reaching her "full potential"—she knows she can be more social if she wants or needs to be, but she also knows that her true calling is to use her strengths as an introvert and accept herself for who she really is.

End scene.

So, as you can see, creating yourself doesn't always end up the way you think it will. For some people, being more out-going, for example, takes a lot of courage, but once they start doing it, they realize that it just feels right—this was what they were missing! They feel energized and alive. This was the person they were supposed to be all along; they just never had the opportunity to try it out. For other people, like Sally, once they try it for a while, they realize that they are just exhausted if they do it all the time. They miss their time alone, and they realize how valuable it is for them to have that time to reflect. Sally is an example of someone trying out a quality that she always wished she had, but then she realized that the reason she never was that way was because it wasn't her True Self. And that's okay.

When You Find Your True Self

While Sally struggled with how outgoing she wanted to be, you might have a different focus as you work through this section of the book—for example, how assertive to be, how busy to be, what goals you want, what fears to face, what skills you want, what relationships to pursue, how independent to be, how vulnerable to be, how brave to be, or how expressive to be. Your goals and your journey may be the same as Sally's, or they may be very different.

If you find yourself in a situation where you try a personality experiment like Sally did and realize that you don't feel better or more *you* after all, take some time to reflect on why you think you have to be a certain way. Ask yourself, *Why is it important to be that way?* After you think about this, if you find you are still struggling with getting through this journey and feeling good about yourself, it might be worthwhile to flip back to Personal Yield Theory: You're You for Good Reasons (part 1, chapter 3).

Fear not, this will all help in the long run. As you surely understand at this point, liking yourself is the key to confidence, which is the key to resiliency and to fulfillment. So no matter who you are, or who you discover your True Self to be, that is the right person. You are the right person. You are good enough.

Steps to Your True Self

The Journey Begins

You probably knew this was coming, but it's definitely time for pen and paper again. Yay! And just to make things interesting, let's also go dig out those lists we created back in part 2 of the book—this is the time to use them again! I hope you took that nugget of advice and kept them somewhere safe! You should have four lists:

1. Who you are

2. Who you want to be

3. Who other people want you to be (who you're "supposed" to be, according to others)

4. What you like about yourself

Did you grab those lists? Okay, great. These will now serve as your guidelines to creating yourself. Take a moment and jot down the list number at the top of each page (that is, your "who you are" list will be list 1, "who you want to be" will be list 2, and so on). Now I want you to look at lists 1 and 4 and compile a baseline of things you want to "keep." These are the things about yourself that you currently like and want to "keep" going forward. This new baseline list will have things like "good listener" or "creative" or "good morals" that are the awesome bits about you. Go ahead! Compile your baseline list. Remember how patient I am! I will wait.

Are ya done? Good!

Okay, once you're done, this is now your baseline and you may label it as such—"Baseline." Now I want you to take some time to enjoy these things that you already are! Check out that list! There's so much good about you. I can tell! I know, I know, I don't even know you! But remember, I know this: you've made it this far in reading this book. You're still invested, you're still reading, and you're still working! That means you are truly dedicated, and that speaks volumes about you and your awesomeness. Go, you!

Now from your lists 2 (who you want to be) and 3 (who other people want you to be/who you're "supposed" to be), are there any things that you'd like to add to your repertoire? Are there things that you would like to be part of your baseline list of who you want to be in the future, that you want to work to add into your life? We are going to put some of these things together to make your "goals" list. To help pick some items for your "goals" list, think about some questions like these to see if any of them fit you:

Do you sometimes wish you got better grades in school?

Would you like to have a few more friends or talk to more people?

Would you like to get involved in some more activities?

Do you wish that you were more organized?

Do you wish you were more open with people?

Would you like to learn a skill that you always wanted to learn but never knew where to start?

Do you wish you were closer with any people in your life?

Do you wish you didn't snap at people quite so often, or that you complimented people a little more frequently?

What do your answers to these questions reveal about what goals you might have? As you think of these goals, make a list of them. Add the heading "Goals" underneath your baseline list. So you should now have two sections on your paper—one that says "Baseline," and one that says "Goals."

Make sure as you're doing this exercise that you're remembering personal yield theory and acknowledging that you're still great as you are now, even as you look at making some new changes. You're the best you that you can be at this point, due to all the things in your life that have brought you to this moment. Remember that your goals are simply there to help you have a direction that you can move in, and to help you build some ideas for how to get there.

Troubleshooting: If you're getting stuck on the step of creating your goals but you know you want to make some positive changes, try this trick. Think for a second of someone you really admire or wish you were more like. What is it about that person that draws you to him or her? Why do you admire about that person? What skills, traits, attitudes, morals, or values does that person have that you wish you had more of? Think about those things, and then take those ideas and write them down as possible goals for yourself.

Create Yourself: Your Personal Résumé

So now comes the "work" part. You have your baseline, and you're happy to be where you are, starting off with yourself, hanging out with yourself, and excited (but maybe nervous) to work on some of these ideas and goals with yourself. You know that you're going to reflect along the way as you start trying new things to see if this is your True Self, like Sally did.

Now, in the same way as you would collect education, experience, and volunteer opportunities to put on your professional résumé, you are going to collect experiences to help you work toward your personal résumé. You will build experiences to practice the traits and qualities that you would like to continue to develop in yourself.

Each of the following steps is in Sally's story. We will work through Sally's story and the steps below, and then recap at the end. You will then be able to follow these same steps yourself when you get to the point of creating your own personal résumé.

- Step 1: Create a goal.

- Step 2: Talk yourself up with mantras and your True Inner Voice.

- Step 3: Channel the energy of a role model.

- Step 4: Make a plan to try things out.

- Step 5: Think about your "safe zone" for practice.

- Step 6: Fake it till you make it, even if it feels weird.

- Step 7: Give it some time.

- Step 8: Reflect.

So let's go back to Sally's story where she tried to be more outgoing. I'll break the story down now, as promised, so that you can put together a successful plan like Sally did.

Step 1: Create a goal. Sally started by making a goal. She did some self-reflection and thought about some areas that she wanted to develop. She then narrowed her goal down to wanting to be more outgoing. She worked to make it a SMART goal (which will talk about more later on) by giving herself a vision, a timeline, and other specifics.

Step 2: Talk yourself up with mantras and your True Inner Voice. For the "talk yourself up" step, Sally found an inner dialogue that helped her feel confident about trying out new things. She also made sure that she used her compassionate True Inner Voice to boost her confidence, just like the second coach from our example in The Epic Battle of the ICK (part 2, chapter 10). For you, this step of "talking yourself up" could be a mantra that you repeat over and over to yourself, such as, "This might be new and scary, but I can do this; this might be new and scary, but I can do this," or whatever else might speak to you. This step might entail writing yourself a letter of encouragement, keeping it in your wallet or your purse, and reading it back to yourself—or writing this letter in the PositiveU app. It might be recording a video of yourself on your webcam and watching or listening to that video on your iPod when you're walking or on the bus. Connect with your positive list about yourself, (which you may also have stored on the PositiveU app that accompanies this book). Do whatever you think will work for you to talk yourself up!

Step 3: Channel the energy of a role model. Sally then channeled the energy of a role model that she envisioned in her head. She chose a very outgoing person who she thought she might like to be like. She pictured someone who embodied the traits she wanted to see in herself, and imagined what that person might have done, and then she tried to imitate this.

"Channeling the energy of a role model" is about finding someone for yourself who you feel has the traits or qualities you are trying to develop. Maybe this will be a friend, teacher, or coach. By thinking of this person as you embark on your adventures, you can think, *What would _____ do?* Then, when you try out different ways of being to help reach your personal goals, you can envision your role model in your head for inspiration and channel that person's energy. Eventually, you will find a pattern that is all your own. But it helps to have a role model as a starting place to give you some direction.

For instance, if you want to get better grades, and you know that the girl in your second period class who gets really good grades has a tutor and devotes three hours to studying on the weekends, try to emulate what she does. Copy that behavior and see if it works for you. How about if you want to be nicer but aren't sure where to start? Think of that guy from your eighth grade class who just made everyone happy to be around him. What did he say? How did he act? What things did he do that you can try to start to do, or do more of? Also, what are some of the things he *didn't* do or say? Try to do less of those things as well. What about your friend who is really good at karate? What did she do to learn that skill? How can you take those same steps? What attitude does she have about practicing, and how can you try to build this same attitude in yourself?

Find your role model and try to see how well you match up with what he or she does. Try making changes where you see there are differences, and then reflect on how those changes fit you—if it is your True Self to be that way.

Step 4: Make a plan to try things out. Next, Sally made a plan of how she was going to practice her approach to being more outgoing. She did some research and found some student clubs that she felt comfortable attending, and at the same time challenged herself to go somewhere she didn't already know people. She decided that this would be a safe venue to practice some of her new approaches, but challenging enough that she could make some positive changes. She made sure she had the time to invest in the process, and that she would not have to stop partway through, before she really gave things a shot. These are all things to keep in mind as you look at making your own plan—how can you set yourself up for the greatest chance at success? (For more on how to do this, see the "Create Your Own Story" section a bit later in this chapter. That section elaborates on goals.)

Step 5: Think about your "safe zone" for practice. Another key point about Sally's plan is that she decided to practice new traits or qualities around people that she didn't know yet. There's a bit of logic to her particular approach; let's look at why Sally chose her safe zone as she did.

If you think about it, the first time you meet people, you have no idea who they are. You essentially wait for them to show you who they are through their words, body language, and actions. Thus, when you're around people that you don't know yet, those people don't have any preconceived notions about who you are or who you "should" be. This allows you to create yourself right in front of their eyes. And they won't know the difference, because they believe that who they see is the real you, right from the start. Why would they think otherwise? Sometimes this can be an empowering environment to try out different versions of yourself. That being said, sometimes people feel most comfortable around their closest friends and allies, and prefer to let their friends know their plan so that they can get support as they work toward their goals. Either of these approaches is good, or you can make up your own twist. There's no right way—just the right way for *you*!

Step 6: Fake it till you make it, even if it feels weird. The next step Sally took was to use the "fake it till you make it" approach. Sometimes, when trying out new approaches, ideas, or attitudes, you won't feel like yourself at first. This is normal! Remember, just because something feels weird doesn't mean it's wrong. It's just different! Sometimes it can even feel like acting at first, because you've never done some of these things before. That's what change is all about—new things that don't yet feel like they're "you!" The "fake it till you make it" approach gives you time to accept that although you may feel fake at first, if you keep "faking it," at some point it will shift into feeling normal. For instance, if we look back at the way Sally used this approach, it was largely about channeling her role model. She acted like she thought that person would have acted, channeled that energy, and even though it felt "fake" at first, she kept it up until it felt more natural to act that way and until she found her own groove.

Remember the old shoe metaphor and how weird it feels to wear new shoes until they are broken in and you get used to how they feel. Remember also the arm crossing exercise, and how weird it can feel to change a habit when you first try to make a change. But it comes, even if it feels weird and even though it takes more energy to get started. This is what the "fake it till you make it" approach is all about. Your brain might fight it at first, because it is new and different, but it will become natural after a while.

Step 7: Give it some time. Sally spent some time in this role, giving it the experience and energy it deserved. She kept at it for a bit, making sure she really gave this whole process a chance, without making any snap decisions. She remembered that to get a completely clear sense of how she felt, she'd need more than a few experiences under her belt.

Step 8: Reflect. Lastly, after a good amount of time, Sally reflected on how this whole process felt for her. Sally did most of her reflection on her own, just thinking about things and listening to her body and her emotions. To help with this step, other people might like to make a pros and cons list, to journal about it, or to talk with some friends about how they are feeling. After Sally did her reflecting, she decided that she didn't feel this was her True Self after all. But, remembering personal yield theory, Sally knew that she still had built some skills along the way that were going to be helpful for her in future scenarios.

She knew that this was still a very important step in her overall journey in finding herself and creating herself, and that this was the right outcome for her in the end.

There you have it! You now have your guide to the steps to take to create the version of yourself that you've always wanted. It's just about time to get started on them; but first, let's look more at making goals.

Create Your Own Story

Now you know Sally's story of trying out some traits of being more outgoing. But maybe you have a different goal than Sally. Of course, your story might look very different from Sally's. How can you translate your goal into a plan, like Sally did? As promised, here is the part about how to set yourself up for success through your goals, which can help you with step 4 ("Make a plan to try things out") above.

There is a good way and a not-so-good way to create a goal. For instance, having a goal like "I'm going to eat healthier" maybe isn't going to be as helpful as it could be toward achieving that goal, because what does achieving that goal look like? How do you know if you're making progress? It helps to break the goal down into more detail so that you can measure it and achieve it. Perhaps saying, "I'm going to eat at least one vegetable every day" is a good place for you to start. This is a better goal than the vague "I'm going to eat healthier," because in this second case, you can tell if you stay on track. Some of you may recognize this approach to goal-setting from school, referred to as SMART goals—specific, measureable, attainable, relevant, and timely. (There are some variations as to what the letters stand for, but I'm going to use these; I like them the best and I think they are most relevant for our topic.) Let's look at these pieces and see why they are important to making progress as you plan your "create yourself" journey. As we look at each of these elements, think about how you can maybe shift or change the goals you currently have so they fit this model. This will help you to get on track to successfully make the changes you really want to make to like yourself even more.

Specific: You want to know specifically what you are trying to accomplish—flimsy ideas of improvement aren't going to help you achieve that goal. A vague "I want to be a better person" isn't going to help you get to that place—wherever "that place" is. What does a "better person" look like? What does he do? You want to be clear about what a "better person" is to you. Maybe you really mean that you want to be a *nicer* person. Then you have to define what "nicer" looks like, or if it has any actions associated with it. You need some definitions to be able to reach a concrete, specific goal.

Measureable: Your goals have to be measureable so you know if you are on track. You have to be able to measure your progress. You want to have a few benchmarks that you can check in on along your journey. For example, to say "I want more friends" is not easily measurable, because how many friends are "more?" Four? Fourteen? What's the goal? And when do you want to accomplish this by? To say instead "I want three more friends by the end of the school year" is something that you can measure. You can check in on your progress and change your approach if you find you aren't on target for your goal.

Attainable: Let's be realistic about our goals. A goal like "I will play the hardest guitar song ever written by next week" probably isn't the most attainable goal in the world if you've never played guitar before. Make your goal realistic in the grand scheme of life. You know your strengths and the realities of the world around you, so pick your goals accordingly. Stay on your self-time continuum. (If you want a refresher on the self-time continuum, flip back to that section in Daily Facets of You—chapter 16 in part 2!) Also, unlikely goals like "I want to be a millionaire in a year" are probably off the list here so take off winning the lottery. In contrast, an example of an attainable goal would be to learn to play the basic chords on guitar in your first three months of lessons.

Relevant: A goal also has to be relevant to an overall picture or the grand scheme of your life. If your immediate goal is to "get three facial piercings this year" but your overall goal is to become more professional to prepare for your budding career, then your goals maybe aren't lining up to the big picture that you want. Make sure your small goals line up with what you want in your life. For instance, if you want to become a veterinarian, your goal may be to get a volunteer position at a local humane society. You want to invest your time in things that are important to you in the grand scheme.

Timely: You also want to give yourself enough time to get something done, but not so much time that you can easily procrastinate and put something off. This part is about picking a good time frame to achieve your goal. For instance, to say "I want to be able to do ten push-ups by next week" if you currently can't even do one push-up is not a good example of a timely goal because that time frame is unrealistic for building up the necessary muscle and strength. The goal is attainable, but not in that time frame. On the flip side of the coin, the goal "I want to be able to do ten push-ups in the next three years" isn't a very timely goal either because you have given yourself way too much time to get something done. Pick a time frame that is going to be achievable but also challenging so that you are motivated to continue working toward your goal.

The Robot Technique

Now that your goals are made and you've made sure they are SMART, and you've put some thought into some creative ways to start achieving these goals in your life, it's challenge time—start today! But everyone knows that getting started is usually the hardest part of all this.

You have a plan. You're feeling ready. You want to work on that plan. But—sometimes you can get stuck taking that first step. It's the hardest step to take! In fact, in most things in life, the first step is always the most difficult. A good visualization is to imagine a giant boulder that you have to move from one spot to another—how do you move it? You have to start pushing, and that can be really hard at first. It's so heavy, and it's really intimidating to get started. But once you finally dig in and push as hard as you can, you get that boulder moving. And once it's moving, it gains momentum and keeps rolling in the direction that you started pushing. It becomes so much easier! The first push was the hardest part. But how do you start that push when the boulder seems so large and intimidating?

The solution: the robot technique. This handy technique, which I came up with, can also be helpful with getting up in the morning, getting homework done, or doing your chores. For anything that is hard to get started on, this is your tool. It's a souped-up version of a similar task-oriented technique known as "chunking." Chunking is when you break things down into smaller parts so that you can work through a larger task a little bit at a time and not feel as overwhelmed with the overall size of the task. For instance, if you have to write a paper, chunking tells you to first focus only on the introduction, then move on to your first paragraph, and so on, until you finish up only focusing on the conclusion. One piece at a time, the whole thing gets completed.

The robot technique is similar in that it breaks things down into smaller parts like chunking does, but at the same time this technique helps to override the part of your brain (usually your ICK) that complains about having to do something it doesn't want to do. It overrides the voice that can fill you with doubts, fear, questions, lack of motivation, and anxiety when you're about to try something new—like this challenge! When this inner dialogue gets really loud, it can be hard to move— literally! You can be paralyzed with these churning thoughts. You get stuck. Enter the robot technique.

Let's use a very simple scenario to demonstrate how this works: having to do the dishes. You are sitting on the couch in the basement, watching TV, knowing you have to get the dishes done. But they are all the way upstairs. You are so comfy on your couch, and dishes suck. You really don't want to do them, but you know you have to. Your brain tries to talk you out of doing them, and you try to fight back. You try really hard to talk yourself into it, but it's just not working. And the whole time that you are having this argument in your brain, you end up just sitting on the couch, feeling miserable, fighting with yourself, and nothing gets done.

Here's what to do next. You *stop* thinking. Yes, that's right. You stop. You stop trying to reason and argue or talk yourself into doing the dishes. You strictly take action. You halt the thoughts by literally saying out loud (or in your head) "Stop. Just robot." This might make you giggle, and so it should. And that will help you. Giggling is good. It breaks the tension you were creating with yourself. Then visualize yourself as a little person inside your head controlling your robot body—this happens a lot in cartoons. There's a little person at the helm in the brain controlling the body of the robot with switches and levers. You get to be that little person in control at the helm in your own brain. Then think of the smallest possible action necessary to get yourself to do the dishes. What would this step be? What buttons and levers do you push in your brain from your position at the helm?

If you said, "Walk up the stairs," I say, good try, but think smaller. If you said, "Get off the couch," I say go even smaller. Yes, smaller. Here's how it works. You focus on the smallest step possible. As small as tightening your leg muscles so that they move out from under you. As small as placing both feet on the floor. As small as pushing your body up using the armrest of the couch so you are sitting vertically. As small as pushing your hands off the seat of the couch and pressing your weight into your legs. Do you see the pattern? If you had to direct a robot how to get off a couch and up the stairs to do the dishes, you would have to give these tiny, detailed instructions. Then, when your brain is busy processing these tiny orders and trying to think of the next smallest step, you don't even have time to argue with yourself. Before you know it, you are up the stairs, you've turned on the water, and you've started the dishes. You pushed the boulder, it started moving, and you just kept going after that.

You can also use this with your plan to create yourself. Perhaps you know that you want to practice talking to people more, but when it comes to the moment to start speaking, you freeze. Inside your head, you start to question if you should really do it, that maybe it's not the right time, and so on and so on. Just robot. Just think about opening your mouth. Then take a breath in. Then open your mouth. Then start pushing the air from your lungs out and start to speak the first word you were going to say. Suddenly, you've started talking, and now you just have to keep going with it! Just like the boulder. Once you take that first step, you'll just keep rollin'!

So now you are ready! Get out your list of goals, your plan of how to put them into action, and take the leap! Robot your way through it when you need to, and try some new things! Get even better at old things! Talk yourself up, support yourself compassionately, and be your own best friend!

Reflection Basics

You may want to take a few weeks off from reading this book to get some of this goal-building stuff under your belt. This may help you digest everything you've been reading and thinking about. I particularly suggest you revisit Personal Yield Theory: You're You for Good Reasons (part 1, chapter 3); it will make even more sense to you now that you've learned so much more about yourself. Perhaps try out some of the things we have been talking about up to this point and track what works for you and what doesn't. But if you're keen and you want to keep on reading right now so that you know what to do next, I'm going to continue writing from here as if you've done some trial and error on some of your personal goals. I'll write as if you've now moved into the "reflection" phase in step 8 of the "Create Yourself: Your Personal Résumé" section.

It's time to evaluate how you feel now that you've tried some things out. The first thing, of course, is to make sure you account for the "weird" feeling or the "imposter" feeling. Like we talked about—many times now, so I hope you've really got this one down pat!—these are normal responses when trying out new things, and these feelings can often take a while to subside. Don't let this be your reason for giving up. Keep thinking about your ICK, and make sure it's not getting a foothold in your head as you venture forward. Then, when you think you've had enough time to really practice your goals, make sure you reflect like Sally did and see if you like the direction that things are going. Are these changes making you feel better about yourself and helping to make you into the *you* that you want to be? If not, why not? What might be missing? How might you get back on track? Sometimes it takes a bit of trial and error to find what works best for you in the long run. Keep reflecting. Remember to like yourself along the way as you work toward your personal goals.

One way to self-reflect is to write down your thoughts and experiences in a journal or on your computer. Sometimes when you put your thoughts and emotions in writing, you find them a lot easier to make sense of. This is because when we write ideas down and our eyes have to reread those words, we can filter the thoughts all over again. This also happens when we say things out loud and our ears hear the words again; we filter them a second time. When we filter our thoughts as if the information came from an external source, using our eyes or ears, we can actually access a different secondary filter system in the brain.

Remember when we talked about your True Inner Voice and the fact that if you were in a burning building and your inner voice told you to get out, you wouldn't normally stop to consider if it was right or not? This same phenomenon applies here, too. When we think something inside our own head, our brain treats it as a true thought from our inner voice and trusts it as a default. When the thought stays in our inner circle of brain thoughts, it can only access that one level of analytic power, which isn't the strongest. However, if we receive information externally, we usually stop to analyze it and then we use a different filter system. For instance, if someone else told us to get out of a building because there was a fire, usually we would stop to look around and see if they were messing with us or not. We would check if there really was a fire or how other people were reacting. We filter statements more thoroughly when they come from an external source, and our brain processes this information in a different way.

This is the number one reason why talking to a friend, family member, or counselor often works—we tend to do a lot of the thinking and figuring things out ourselves when we say something out loud! When we hear ourselves speak, we think about things in a new way. This is called "talk therapy"—the simple act of talking about something can help you make sure of it by helping you access this secondary analytic filter.

As I mentioned earlier, you can also do this privately by typing or writing out your thoughts and emotions, and then rereading what you wrote. When you reprocess the thoughts as you read, you might gain some clarity on how you feel overall. This can help you to see if some of your fears and anxieties aren't that overwhelming after all, or it can help you see something from all angles.

You can write out your process and reflections on these creating yourself experiments, and then log next to it how you think you are doing, and how it feels. You can track how much time you have spent at something, and reflect on if it seems like a reasonable amount of time for that new weird feeling to have mostly worn off. Without tracking all this and writing it all down, you might think that you have been practicing something for *ages* when in fact you may have only been at it for a few hours altogether. With this tool of journaling, you can make sure you stay on track and continue to reflect on how you really feel about the whole process. Here are some key questions to ask yourself as you reflect:

Have I given this enough time to be successful?

Have I run into any problems with my plan that might be influencing how I feel?

Is my ICK taking over again and making me feel insecure?

Am I happy with the progress I am making?

Should I change anything about my goals?

Do I feel better now that I am finally trying these things?

Is the feedback that I'm getting from people changing how I feel? Is this a good thing, or a bad thing?

Do I need to alter my approach?

Do I feel more comfortable or less comfortable over time as I try these new things?

Have I been using my positive compassionate inner voice?

Have I been encouraging and supportive of myself, even when things have been difficult?

You might also have some questions you think you should ask yourself that are unique to your own situation. As you think of good questions that will help you to reflect on your progress or help you to take stock of how far you have come, write them in a journal and then come back to them over time. Keep at it, and keep that journal handy!

20

Vulnerability 101

The Ultimate Truth

So now you've worked on some goals that you have for yourself, and through your work at achieving those goals, you've explored some skills, traits, experiences, or other aspects of your personality as you learned more about yourself. You're getting closer to finding and creating your True Self. Through your work on these goals, you've found ways to make some positive or meaningful changes in your life. These might only be small changes in safe places so far—and that's normal. Just like Sally tried out being more outgoing in some social clubs where she didn't already know people (so she could practice her skills without fear of judgment from people that she cared about), maybe you have been making changes in your life in safe ways as well. And that's great! It's the perfect place to start. You've done a lot of work if you've gotten this far, and you've put a lot of thought into this process. You've now figured out who you are and who you want to be, and you are well on your way toward getting comfortable with your True Self. So now it's time to show this off to the world.

This creation of your True Self is probably close to your heart because of how much time and effort you've put into it. Thus, letting people see this version of yourself can be scary. What if they don't like you? What if some people don't support the changes you are making? Now that you've spent all this time and energy creating this person and opening yourself up to your full potential, you may find it very threatening to show this True Self to everyone. This is where our conversation on vulnerability begins.

Vulnerability is a fact of life. I had originally written "a *simple* fact of life," but I took out the "simple" because it actually is quite a complicated topic with complicated emotions surrounding it. Vulnerability is the root of fear, insecurity, and defensiveness. It's also the root of pretending to be someone or something that we are not. Being vulnerable is a scary thing, and most of us do just about anything we can to protect ourselves from getting hurt by minimizing our vulnerability.

We do things like only post happy and exciting pictures of ourselves on social media, making sure that we look good in every tagged photo. We only tell stories of things that we are comfortable sharing, keeping our deepest truths to ourselves or only sharing them with our loved ones. We lie when people ask how we are doing, and we never ever share our biggest insecurities outside of our inner circle of most sacred trusted allies. Sometimes we don't share them with anyone at all. These are normal and common things that we do, and they can truly keep us safe from unwanted assumptions, advice, or judgments from others. But sometimes, left unchecked, these behaviors can keep us isolated and feeling like no one knows who we truly are. In more intense scenarios, they can keep us locked behind walls that we build to keep others out. The problem is this: those same walls that keep others out can also lock us inside.

To avoid vulnerability, many of us walk around with a metaphorical mask on. This is the "safe" version of ourselves that we feel we can allow other people to see. This version is often socially acceptable, usually nonthreatening, and generally agreeable. Sometimes this mask has a tough, "don't mess with me" exterior. People choose different masks for different reasons.

This mask is usually fine for getting through superficial daily interactions where authenticity isn't really necessary to function normally. A masked version of yourself is usually safe because if someone doesn't like *that* version of you, you don't feel threatened. Your True Self wasn't the one that was challenged. It wasn't the *real* you, so that part of you is still safe. It's fine if people don't like your mask since it only serves to protect your True Self, like a type of armor.

The real threat comes if other people decide they don't like your True Self. That's a hit to the core. That's your soft, vulnerable, smooshy spot. It hurts a lot when it gets hit, unlike your hardened outer mask. So we keep our True Selves hidden from everyone except the most trusted people in our lives—or sometimes we keep them hidden from everyone. We protect our soft spot.

The danger here is that you can get so comfortable with your mask, your shell, and your walls, and so scared of someone not liking your True Self, that you stay permanently behind your mask and hide your True Self from everyone. You never take the mask off, and this can isolate you and keep you from growing as an individual, or truly connecting on a deeper, more authentic level with people around you.

Because it is scary to show people your True Self, you keep secrets and you hide your real thoughts, feelings, desires, and emotions so that no one can hurt you. However, the trick is that showing these things to people and being vulnerable is the only path to real, honest human connection. And we, as humans, were not built to survive without this real, honest connection with others. A lack of true connection to others has been linked to depression and even suicide (Bearman and Moody 2004; Laird, Bridges, and Marsee 2013; Prinstein 2007). While we are on that topic, if you ever have thoughts of hurting yourself or taking your life, you need to tell someone right away. Whether it is your friend, teacher, parent, counselor, religious leader, or relative, you need to say it out loud and talk to someone today. You are not going to get in trouble or get yelled at—and if you ever think that you will get yelled at, try calling one of the local suicide help lines in your area instead. The phone numbers are easy to find online, and the people that work on these help lines really want to hear your story. I've worked on one—it makes our time worthwhile when we get to hear from someone like you and possibly even help you with whatever you might be going through. It gets boring when no one calls to talk to us! We really do want to talk with you. There absolutely is help out there, but you need to be a bit vulnerable and reach out to tell someone today so that you can get connected with the right people to help you through it all. Please. I could write a whole other book on this, but that's for another day. Reach out, tell someone, and allow yourself to be helped. You deserve it. Future You will thank Present You *sooo* much! The same message applies if you know anyone else who might be feeling this way; reach out and tell someone today. It's always better to have a friend who is a bit mad at you for telling someone about how she feels than to have a friend who isn't around anymore.

Okay, thanks for listening to that last bit—it was important. Now let's go back to our discussion about masks. Let's review. We are now stuck in a catch-22 with this idea of your mask versus your True Self. If you show people your True Self, they could hurt you. Your soft spot would be vulnerable. But if you never show your True Self, you will never connect with anyone in a meaningful way. And meaningful connection is the only way to truly live. You can't survive in a healthy long-term way without meaningful human connection. So with vulnerability comes risk. And risk is scary—hence, the catch-22.

However, if we really think about it, there really is only one viable option, and that is to take the risk. To be vulnerable. To put yourself out there. You can do it in small steps. You can take off bits and pieces of your mask at a time. Try it out. Get comfortable. Take the risk. Otherwise, without this honest connection to others, you're not going to get a whole lot out of life. For an even deeper discussion about vulnerability, I suggest you check out some of Brené Brown's work, especially her TED Talks online.

So now that you know that this scary vulnerability of taking off your mask and exposing your soft spot is a necessary risk—a risk you must take to live a meaningful and full life—it's time to steel yourself and take some risks with the bright, shiny, new True Self you've been working on. It's time to allow yourself to be seen. That being said, if your soft smooshy spot is going to come out in the open, it's probably a good idea if we spend some time talking about what to do if you do get negative feedback. It makes sense to understand how to handle this risk.

But the answer is *not* to run and hide behind your mask! Stay awhile. Let's figure out how to respond instead.

Winning the Vulnerability War

As mentioned, if you show your True Self and you get negative feedback, you may be tempted to choose option A, which is to run, hide, and revert back to the "safe" version of yourself. Not you! You've worked too hard to run back and hide your amazing True Self behind that old mask again! So what do we do instead? Abandon all friends, family, and relatives who react to us in a way we don't like? That's probably not a great idea either.

This is where "assertive defense of the self" comes into play, originally formulated by Christine Padesky (1997). This is option B. This is great practice for just about every area of your life. It follows the "what if/I can" approach we talked about earlier in the book. (See the section "Follow the Fear: Change 'What If' to 'I Can'" in chapter 12, The Tiny Grain of Truth.) So, what if you show off your True Self that you've been working on, the self that is more agreeable and less argumentative, and "they" say you are a pushover? What if you've been working on being more confident, and "they" say that you are conceited? To deal with these comments, here's a trick for you: develop a self-confidence script. Whatever negative things you fear that people will say about you, come up with a response in advance. Rehearse that response in your head and then be ready to use it if or when it's needed.

Let's say you fear that as you become more confident, people will misinterpret this and think you've become conceited. This is one of the reasons you have stayed behind your mask for so long; people might think that a more vocal you is a more conceited you! Thus, as you start to venture out with your more confident self, the vulnerable part of you fears that someone will label you or judge you. Let's see how an exchange between you and this judgmental person might go.

Other Person: Wow. You've become so conceited lately. You are so full of yourself!

Interesting. That's quite the judgment. But it's been thrown out there, and we all know that there are people in this world who can just be mean. We can handle this. Let's think about it. What could you say back to that? What would be an assertive response that defends your True Self?

Now, you want to be *assertive*, not aggressive. (This isn't called "aggressive defense of the self.") That means no name calling, no attacking, and no yelling. What could you say that asserts yourself and defends who you've become, while not attacking the other person? I want you to seriously think about an answer before you read the possibilities that I've come up with, because at some point, you will want to come up with some ideas on your own. That way, when you don't have this book in your hands, you can still do these things in your own head. I have faith in you! Remember, there are always multiple "right" answers for something like this. Okay. Think. Go! (Waits.) Good?

Okay, I wish I could hear what you've come up with, but unfortunately this book is a one-way channel, so you're going to have to just read mine and check if yours is somewhat similar. Let's start our script again.

Other Person: Wow. You've become so conceited lately. You are so full of yourself!

(You pause to think—you give yourself some time to remember all the different facets of yourself in order to check that it is not just Angry You talking. You think you are in a good place, so you take a breath and respond.)

You: Actually, I think I've developed a lot more confidence lately. I'm feeling a lot better about myself, and I'm sorry you see my confidence as being conceited. I personally think it is an improvement, and I'm proud of the work I've done.

Now, of course, you can always decide how much you need to reveal about yourself depending on whom you are talking to. There are some people in your life worth responding to with more detail and some people who you don't need to give as much energy to. If it is a close friend or relative, it might be worth getting into a discussion, if you are ready. If it's a petty person at school who you know is rude to everyone, you can choose how much energy you want to put into your response. A simple "I'm sorry you feel that way" might be enough in that case.

Let's try another one. In this next example, you've been working on being less direct and more go-with-the-flow because you had been feeling like you had too many conflicts in your life:

Other Person: You've really become a pushover lately. You've got no spine.

What could you say to that? Think about it a bit again before you read on. (Waits.) Okay, maybe you respond something like this:

You: *(After taking a self-reflective pause.)* I actually
               think I've become a lot better at working
               in groups lately, and I really like this new
               side of myself. I haven't been getting into as
               many arguments, and I enjoy spending more
               time listening to other people's opinions. I'm
               sorry you see that as me being a pushover,
               but personally I think I've been developing
               better teamwork skills.

Do you see the pattern? As you think of what you might encounter from someone who questions or judges your True Self, write down the fear as a verbal attack from a stranger or friend—such as "you're so conceited" or "you've really become a pushover." You can write this in a journal, on your tablet or phone, or even just think about it in your head—however you work best. Then, once you have the fear written down, come up with what you might say to that person if she ever said something like that to you in real life.

This exercise can prepare you to both show your True Self to people and to be more vulnerable, because you will feel like you can defend yourself and your choices no matter what is said to you. You will feel stronger and more confident to face whatever comes your way.

Even if you never say any of these things out loud, you can always say them to yourself. For instance, sometimes we suspect that someone is silently judging us, even if that person never actually says something mean to our face. This can damage our confidence even though we are never actually confronted by someone. We may never have to face that person in real life, but the silent conversation in our own heads can be upsetting. But fear not! You can still face this person and keep yourself strong. You can rehearse this type of script in your head *as if* that person spoke to you. For instance, if you get the feeling that someone is judging you as being conceited, whether you just get "that feeling" or you see it in her eyes, but she doesn't say anything out loud to you, you should still go through the above assertive defense-of-the-self script in your head. Pretend she did say it out loud, and then, in your head, respond to her. You can have a silent conversation with yourself in this format to help you get through those moments of questioning and doubting yourself so that you can come out victorious on the other side! This is one way that you can help to keep yourself from going back and hiding behind your mask when you are questioned about aspects of your True Self.

Some of you may have noticed that these conversations are similar to those that you have with your ICK—when that voice inside your head is just your own ICK trying to bring you down. This process is also similar to the one for following your fear. Whatever the fear is, follow it! Turn "what if" into "I can." Track down the fear and come up with a solution. What would you say? What would you do? By coming up with these answers, you will feel like you can handle anything. You can build on all of these skills from earlier in the book to feel more confident and assertive in all of your relationships.

21

Romantic Relationships

Liking Yourself in a Relationship

Now that you've made it through the past, the present, and now partway through the future, you are finally ready to look at romantic relationships. If you are one of those people who has flipped to this section first before reading the rest of the book (because, hey, relationships are pretty interesting), by all means, come join us. But bear in mind that you will probably be most successful and happy if you also check out the rest of this book before diving too deeply into this chapter.

As they say, you have to like yourself before someone else can like you. Not a hard and fast rule, but definitely something to think about. You don't always want to have to get your validation externally (that is, to only be happy when someone *else* likes you), which, as we've learned, can be a temporary situation—breakups do happen! Ideally, you first want to be comfortable with yourself and like yourself. That way, even if a relationship ends, you can be stable because you know that you are still happy with the number one person in your life—you!

So let's look now at how to make sense of relationships in terms of confidence and liking yourself.

How to Get a Relationship

Interestingly enough, this has a lot to do with chapter 20, Vulnerability 101. There are many "ways to get a guy (or girl)" as *Cosmo* or *Maxim* might tell you, but (and I know this might come as a shock) the "tricks of the trade" really are just that—tricks. We don't really want tricks, because they don't last. Although they are fun to read about, and they provide some solid entertainment on airplanes and on road trips, they don't tend to pan out as well in real life as the magazines make you believe. This is because these tricks are not your True Self. Therefore, if you get the guy by using "tricks," you've gotten that guy to fall for someone who isn't the real you. Then you've signed yourself up to be someone different from who you really are in that relationship, and that's probably not going to last. You're going to be very busy keeping up an act, and that can get exhausting.

If you want something substantial, you're going to want to be real. This starts with what is known as flirting, which, in all honesty, could just be called "A Conversation with Energy and Intention." That's probably too long of a title to catch on as mainstream lingo, but let me explain why it works. The difference between a normal conversation and flirting is the energy and intention.

In a regular conversation (for example, at work or with an acquaintance), your energy level is usually lower and less intense, and you send out energy signals of "Hey, friend." With flirting, your energy level and your focus on the other person are higher, and you project confidence, positive regard, and attraction outward to that person. At the same time, you watch and wait for positive signals from that person to be returned. In simple terms, you hint through your body language, energy, and your conversation that you like the other person, and see if that person returns those hints.

More than magazines will ever tell you, the number one trick to flirting and "getting relationships" is confidence. Confidence, of course, stems from liking yourself. This is why this section is at the end of the book—because now that you're on your way to liking yourself, hopefully that confidence thing is getting easier.

Now, there are one hundred different ways that *Cosmo* or *Maxim* will break down this confidence thing into "tricks." But to prove my point, if you read between the lines of any of these "tricks" or any of this "advice," it all comes back to confidence. We'll go through a couple of examples so that you can see these tricks aren't just about temporarily making some changes to how you act so that you can snag someone, but that they all lead to the overall point of this book—that permanently and truly liking yourself, and the confidence that comes with that, is the real key to this whole mystery.

Take, for instance, this gem from one of those dating advice columns: "Girls don't like guys that are too needy. Play hard to get." (Yes, I just Googled some of these pieces of advice—this is what is out there!) Well, that's weird advice in a way, and it certainly could be worded more delicately, but it's probably also something we've all heard before. This is because on some level, it seems to work. Why? How does it work, and how is that linked to confidence? How can we understand the psychology behind this so we don't see it as a "trick" that we have to learn, but know that we can achieve the same outcome by liking ourselves with confidence?

In relation to confidence—and again, this isn't a hard-and-fast rule for everyone, but let's explore the idea—people who are "needy" project outward that they are desperate for attention and approval. If you are desperate for attention and approval, you likely don't give yourself sufficient attention and approval. Often when you don't like yourself enough and don't have enough confidence in yourself to just "know" that people are going to like you and that one day you will find the right person for you, you can come off as being needy or clingy. Searching for external approval is often the result of this internal lack of confidence. Other people don't tend to like that, which we will explore in more detail later on.

For all of the tricks and tips that are out there in magazines and blogs, if you look at each one in depth, you'll start to see the pattern. You can break each one of them down as to how it is really linked to confidence. I could go on with more examples, but next time you find an article about "how to wow him/her" or "get the guy/girl of your dreams," check to see if it has anything to do with confidence. Try these (I just Googled them!): Be funny. Strike up a conversation. Break the touch barrier. Be interesting. Don't cake on makeup (for the ladies). And so on and so on. Code? They all really mean: be confident, be yourself. These are not temporary tricks and games that you need to learn, but instead these tips show that finding success in flirting and in finding relationships actually stems from an overall deep confidence in liking your True Self. Doing these "tricks" for a day won't get you the relationship you are looking for (at least not a sustainable one), but having a lifelong appreciation for yourself and having confidence in yourself will.

Being Your True Self with Confidence

Okay, we're going to get deep for a second. We're going to get into the real stuff about confidence, your True Self, and relationships, and why this combination is so important. Ready?

People are attracted to others with confidence because this is an indication that they are willing and available to open up and connect. The human soul searches for a true, meaningful connection. So when we see someone who opens up with confidence, we are attracted to the possibility that we can engage safely with this person on a deeper, more vulnerable level.

If someone resists opening up and connecting with others, for whatever reason, that person's True Self is not readily seen, and because of that, the chances that people will be attracted to that person's energy are much smaller. People often only like, appreciate, and love what they can see, so you might as well show your True Self to the world and let the attraction come to you. People are attracted to confidence because it indicates that you are ready and comfortable to open up and connect in a meaningful way.

Further, people can often detect fraud and deception on an energy level. If you try to present yourself as someone different than your True Self, or even if you are standoffish and don't allow people in, then you're hiding a part of the truth of who you are, even if you don't mean to. When people can't see that truth about you, they become somewhat reserved and skeptical about you. This is because what you show them is not as emotionally safe as something they can see in someone else right away. For other people to open up to you, they need to feel a sense of safety and security. If they do not feel safe and secure with you, they will not open up, and then a true connection will never be made.

For people to feel most safe and secure around you, being your True Self is one of the best tools at your disposal. Even if not everyone will like your True Self, you will have a much higher success rate of people liking you and connecting with you than if you are closed off. This is because those who can see your True Self will feel safe, and then if they like you, they will open up to you in return, and this is where a true connection can be made.

Translation? If you hide your True Self and don't open up with confidence, you are only hurting yourself in the end. Even though vulnerability goes up when you are your True Self (because if someone doesn't like you, it hurts in that soft spot instead of bouncing off your walls and your mask), at the end of the day, it's worth the risk. Even though the possibility increases that more people may not like the *real* you (instead of just your mask), you will always have a higher number of people who will respond positively to you because you show confidence and are genuine. It still won't be everyone, but it will be the right people. You will hurt a little more when you are rejected, but you don't really want people around who don't like your True Self anyway. The people who are attracted to you and want to spend time with you when you are your True Self will be the ones that really matter. Remember the saying: "Be who you are and say what you feel, because those who mind don't matter, and those who matter don't mind."

Think about it. If you play games, if you try to be someone else, if you try to make someone else happy by changing who you are, all you are doing is signing yourself up for a lifetime of having to be someone that you aren't. If you are your True Self, the people who will respond to you will stick around because of that meaningful connection with you. They will like you because they know who you really are, not who you pretend to be. And you won't have to work so hard all the time because you won't have to put on an act. You just get to "be." And they will like you anyway! How cool is that?

So if you get hung up on "that guy" or "that girl" who doesn't seem to like you, ask yourself this—because you now like yourself (or you are on your way!), why would you want to be with someone who doesn't like you? You deserve someone who likes you back! Otherwise, what's the point? You can't change someone else's mind (unless you play a game and pretend to be someone you aren't, which we've learned isn't helpful), so clearly that guy or girl who isn't liking you back is not actually the right person for you!

Don't fall for someone's potential—recognize the reality of who someone is and how he or she interacts with the *real* you. Otherwise you will be busy trying to fool that person all the time, or driving yourself nuts over an idea that is not, in fact, reality. Yes, this rule is still true even if "that person" is really pretty, cute, rich, successful, in a band, and so on. It will still be a crap relationship in the end if you don't get to actually be yourself!

22

How to Be Okay with Rejection

Why It's Important

We started to touch on this idea of rejection at the end of the last chapter, but it's important, so let's elaborate. One of the risks, of course, with having confidence and putting your True Self out there is that rejection will occur. This is true for everyone. You may even be struggling right now with some past rejections, or you may be worried about future rejections. Rejections can be embarrassing and hurtful, as we all know. But we've all seen some people who are able to bounce back from rejections and keep on trucking, not feeling worse about themselves. How do they do it? How can we get to that place of self-confidence, too? The first step is to understand rejection and to take out some of the perceived personal judgment. We need to take away the feelings of being attacked or devalued. This is going to be a bit of a touchy subject in a lot of ways, but I'm going to do my best to keep this strictly logical so that you can still see your greatness even in the face of rejection. It will help you remember how to like yourself in all situations.

So now that we're talking about rejection, here are some questions to think about: If you are your True Self, and someone doesn't like you, does that mean there is something wrong with you? Do you have to change everything? Do you have to change anything? No. What if you don't like someone else? Is there something wrong with him? Nope. Someone else out there will find him perfectly intriguing one day; it's just a matter of the right fit.

Though the overall answer to these questions is no, there is always room for a little self-reflection in life. I want to make sure that you don't just go blasting through the world not caring at all what other people think, because self-reflection is important. For instance, did someone not like you because you only talked about yourself the whole time? Some social skill tweaking to change that habit doesn't have to change the core of who you are. If you do get feedback from someone, you can take that feedback in, consider it, and see if it is important to you to make any changes based on it or not. But you can do this without having to feel like you are a failure or that you are worthless. Always remember personal yield theory: once you know better, you can do better. Recognize that even if you'd like to make some changes to yourself or how you act after you reflect on some feedback you've received, this doesn't mean that you are not a good person today. Even if you still have some room to grow, as we all do, this doesn't mean that you aren't worthwhile *today*. You will always be growing, and the person who you are now is just as valuable as the person you will become. This is because you can't become the person you will be in the future without being who you are today. Let me say that again: you can't become the person you will be in the future without being who you are today. So therefore, you're awesome at all times. There's literally no other option. You are worthwhile in every stage of your life, every day, and every moment—the good, the bad, and the ugly. That's the message we're trying to get at here!

The Bell Curve of "Normal"

Let's break the idea of rejection down a bit more by using some examples to help understand attraction. This way, we can understand rejection on a logical level so that we can help to protect our vulnerable little soft spots. We can keep our self-worth linked to our personal qualities instead of looking at strict numbers of people who are interested in us. This conversation will hopefully help you to like yourself in any situation where you might be faced with rejection—in relationships and friendships, including breakups.

We all know every guy out there seems to like Tori, and Tori gets tons of guys. Same with Tyler—all the girls are dying to go on a date with him. What's up with Tori and Tyler? What is working for them? What's the secret? Well, first, they probably have a lot of confidence, plus a somewhat "standardized cultural perception of attractiveness." This phrase refers to what our culture has shaped us to believe is attractive. We've already touched on confidence and why that is important, and we'll shelve the physical attractiveness conversation for a second and come back to it later. What else might these people have that can explain this frenzy of attention that they seem to get?

Beyond the confidence and attractiveness that Tori and Tyler probably have, there is also a cultural bell curve of "normal." In statistics, this is referred to as "normal distribution." This term refers to the pattern in math where there is an "average" category that the highest number of people will fall into, and the further you get away from that average, the fewer the people who will fall into those categories. Check out figure 1 to see what I mean. That figure illustrates the distribution of "normal" (that is, average) heights—in this case, the height of American men. The average height of an adult American man is 5 feet 10 inches, which would be right on the center line in the figure. For the rest of the curve, all the other heights would be distributed from shortest on the left to tallest on the right. There aren't a lot of adult men who are shorter than five feet, and there aren't a lot of adult men that are taller than seven feet, but there are a few. The men that are shorter than five feet will fall in area C on the far left of the curve. The men taller than 7 feet will fall in area C area on the right of the curve. These C areas are the least common or, in the language of statistics, least "normal." The adult men that are a little closer to the average will fall in the B areas on either side of the middle of the curve, indicating that their heights are more common. Then, finally, in the A area of the curve—the most common area—you will find all the men closest to that "normal" average height, probably from about 5 feet 7 inches to about 6 feet 1 inch.

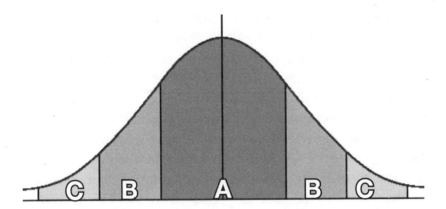

Figure 1. The bell curve of "normal."

This distribution of heights looks like figure 1, which in turn looks like a bell on a graph—that's also where the term "bell curve" comes from. The people who are of average height are then called "normal"—in this case. For this conversation, when I use the word "normal," I refer only to statistical frequency— the "normal" is the average, the top of the bell curve in area A.

We can use the bell curve to illustrate other characteristics as well. For example, some interests and hobbies are more culturally "normal" (that is, more common) and easier to connect to than others. Let's look at interests and hobbies now in order to understand this bell curve of "normal" a bit better. I'm going to use the culture I'm most familiar with in my examples, but feel free to think of some of your own cultural norms if they differ from the ones I use. I'm also going to flip back and forth between male and female references so that you can see how these examples apply to everyone.

Okay, so how many people would probably like a guy who plays soccer, hockey, or football? Sure, lots of people would probably know and recognize those hobbies and would thus be able to connect to and understand that person. This means that a hobby like playing one of those sports would fit under area A on the cultural bell curve of "normal"—that is, most common (see figure 1). There are a lot of people who fall under these categories of sports. Thus, this would likely be an attractive feature of that person, because a lot of people understand it. That increases the "pool of people" who might be interested in pursuing a relationship with that person right away, because other people easily connect to and understand something about him. The height of the graph in area A would then indicate the increased number of people attracted to this quality that a person has, since it is most common.

Now, what about a guy whose hobby is foraging? Do you even know what that is? (Answer: It's going out into nature and gathering edible food resources, largely berries and mushrooms). Maybe not as many people would be instantly attracted to that, or feel that they would fit well with that person's lifestyle, because it's not as common as a hobby (statistically speaking). It would fall out on the edges of the statistical normal distribution bell curve, in the C areas. So for the guy whose hobby is foraging, there might be a smaller initial "pool of people" who would immediately connect to that particular aspect about him. The height of the graph in the C areas indicates the lower number of people who would be immediately connected to and attracted to this aspect about this person. This means that people might not flock to this guy as frequently based on strict numbers of people who have these kinds of uncommon interests, such as foraging. Again, these are not the only aspects of people that others look for regarding relationships, and having a less "common" interest or hobby does not make you *actually* less attractive. Of course there is a much larger picture, but bear with me as we use some simpler examples to explore this idea.

In terms of people who "get" and "relate" to a person right away, based on that person's lifestyle, hobbies, or interests, this means that sometimes you have a larger audience of people who would fit well with you based on the statistical popularity of certain activities or personality traits. When people first meet other people, they look at some of these traits right off the bat to try to make decisions on what types of relationships might be a good fit for them. The bell curve of "normal" can help explain why some people seem to attract more frequent attention from interested parties. This does *not* reflect self-worth, but only statistical norms.

Back to Tori and Tyler—maybe they are good examples of a "normal" bell curve, where they might attract a fairly broad audience. Maybe Tori is a cheerleader (culturally and stereotypically, a lot of people tend to find that attractive in a female), and maybe Tyler is in a band (again, culturally and stereotypically, that seems to be something a lot people find attractive in a male). So, because their hobbies and interests are commonly considered attractive, Tori and Tyler fall at the apex of the bell curve in the A area. For Tori and Tyler, by having greater numbers of people that might be able to connect with them on this bell curve of "normal," they have a higher chance of people being interested in them for a relationship based on strict global numbers. This could begin to explain why so many people flock to them. This example of norms can work with all heterosexual and LGBTQ relationships.

Here's the kicker: this increase in initial numbers of interested parties, on its own, does not guarantee a deep, meaningful connection with someone. These are largely just surface qualities and traits that people base their initial judgments on. They have nothing to do with anyone's overall personality—just the range of people who they might seem to "fit" with superficially. For our purposes in this book, this can help us to understand the frustration that sometimes comes with watching other people like Tori and Tyler get a lot of attention. What makes them so great? Well, sometimes it just comes down to numbers. This is something to remember if you don't happen to have people flocking to you, or if you hang out with a group of people that has a Tori or a Tyler in it. They just might be easier for others to approach based on this cultural bell curve of "normal."

Remember that's only the starting point—even for Tori and Tyler—and it only accounts for initial propositions. Because people start with the more superficial things when deciding if they are interested in pursuing a relationship with another person (because really, there's nowhere else to start), a lot of attraction and rejection just comes down to numbers on a statistical level. This in no way means you have to change who you are, but it can be something to keep in mind if you start to feel like "no one likes you," as you watch Tori and Tyler get all the attention. It also helps to understand rejection if Tori or Tyler rejects *you*, because they have higher numbers of people propositioning them, so they have to reject more people—they can't date everyone, after all.

Understanding Attraction

Okay, let's get back to physical attractiveness. We've now looked a bit at the cultural bell curve of "normal" as it applies to things like hobbies or interests. Now it's time to look at the physical. Do your best to stay with me as we delve into this emotionally charged subject; this one can feel a little more personal, but it's really the same concept as the last section. Let's break it down.

Physical attractiveness can be a lot of different things to a lot of different people, and everyone has different tastes. But just about anyone will attest that, at the end of the day, the most important thing about good looks is the confidence a person has. Confidence encompasses a confident way of speaking, acting, and even dressing. (Just watch a few episodes of *What Not to Wear* to see this in action!) This is why we talked so much about confidence at the beginning of the book! But in addition to confidence, when people first meet each other, that confident body language will also be mixed in with the visual appearance of a person: the physical. When people first meet each other, they are limited to making decisions and assumptions based often on their first initial responses to physical attraction. We all do it.

This is where, either through nature or nurture (that is, what we find attractive physiologically or what we are taught to believe is attractive), there are indeed some things that a larger number of people will commonly tend to consider attractive and be attracted to. For instance, (again, I'm using the culture I am most familiar with), taller, broad-shouldered men are culturally considered to be more attractive, and at this point in time, athletic, bustier women also tend to be considered more attractive. Depending on where you might fall on this cultural bell curve of "normal," you may have more or less people who are naturally attracted to you on first appearances, based on strict "averages." (Again, remember this is a statistical "norm," not a reflection of worth!)

Now, before we all get too discouraged by the state of the world and how judgmental everyone is about external appearance and "There's more to people than just looks!"—I want to stop you there. Of course there's more to people than just looks! Abso-friggin-lutely! People are beautiful in all shapes, sizes, colors, heights, weights, in everything! But there's something to understand about this "normal" bell curve that will help with the confidence and liking yourself bit. Not understanding this bell curve can hold a lot of people back in truly liking themselves when they experience rejection or when they watch other people like Tori or Tyler get more attention. This is because they *do* start to base their self-worth on these numbers, without understanding that these statistics are only superficial. They don't remind themselves that this is not linked to actual value, and in the moment of rejection they forget that there are people out there attracted to *every* type of person, even if it isn't as statistically frequent. Understanding how the numbers work can help you be more resilient if you don't fall into a Tori or Tyler category.

Learning to separate your emotions from why people may or may not be attracted to you is very important, and once you are able to apply the above logic it makes sense, but, emotionally, this category of physical appearance can be tricky to master. In contrast, when it comes to hobbies or lifestyle choices, people don't seem to get too emotionally hurt if someone doesn't find their very interesting but not-so-mainstream hobby of, for instance, foraging, attractive. "Cool, fine, no worries, if it's not for you, it's not for you," you might say to yourself. You would probably be pretty sure that you want someone who likes that about you, anyway, because you like that about you! It really is pretty cool once you learn about it. (I have a friend who does this!) So in this case, emotions don't often get pulled in and you don't think you're a failure, just because someone doesn't really jibe with your foraging thing.

But often when it comes to our physical appearance, we can't separate emotions and logic quite as well. This all comes down to the infamous sentence (or your personal variation of this) "because I'm not _____ enough, no one will ever like me." Insert your favorite word or phrase—skinny, tall, curvy, broad-shouldered, clear-skinned—whatever "it" is you think you "should" or "shouldn't" be. (Remember: Watch out for those "shoulds!") This is a trap. Let's keep delving into this a little further.

Let's replace foraging in the first example from the last section with a physical trait in this example. Let's use height for guys. If a girl isn't attracted to a guy immediately because he "isn't tall enough" and the girl "only dates tall guys," there are two things going on here. First, that girl probably isn't right for that guy because she isn't able to see past this physical trait, or she has her reasons why she doesn't want to see past this physical trait. Therefore, these two people aren't the right match. Second, that girl honestly seems to have a reason why she prefers taller men, and this preference is still a preference, and people are allowed to prefer things. Just like someone might want to have their favorite hobbies match up with their partner, people are also allowed to prefer people that they are honestly attracted to. That's the difference between a friendship and a relationship, after all—attraction and intimacy.

You probably prefer some things, too, if you think about it! Maybe you like girls with tattoos. Maybe you like guys with long hair. Again, this is all a starting place for people when they first meet another person and all they have to go on is the superficial.

But most of these physical traits that the majority of people immediately "prefer" often fit under the bell curve of "normal"—in that they are the most commonly preferred traits across the population. This may be why Tori and Tyler get a lot of attention; maybe they are quite stereotypical in their appearance of what is considered most averagely attractive. This average-ness would increase both Tori and Tyler's initial "pool of people" who might consider them potential partners. This does not mean they are better people, however. In fact, it's largely a case of luck. Let's think about that one.

If there were a sign-up list wherever we are before we are born here on Earth, who would say, "Yes, please, sign me up for the big nose and acne, please!"? These are not things we get to choose about ourselves. So make sure you keep that in mind both when looking for a partner and when being considered as a partner. Most physical traits are not chosen and thus are not reflective of self-worth. You don't get points for something like being tall—you didn't become this way by any personal choices, special skills, or talents. Your DNA set things up that way; it was predetermined. So when you next catch yourself thinking someone is better or cooler than you because of a physical trait that he didn't choose, stop yourself. That is not where real self-worth lies. It lies in someone's morals, values, skills, knowledge, and most of all, actions. I'll repeat: most physical traits are not chosen, thus they are not reflective of self-worth.

The most important thing is to be with someone who likes you for *all* of you, and you remember your confidence and how the right person *is* out there for you. You remember that, because of how awesome you are, you have the confidence to know that just because someone isn't attracted to you for a superficial reason like height, this doesn't have anything to do with your self-worth. If another person does not fit into a relationship puzzle in your life for this reason, that doesn't mean that *no one* ever will. (Watch out for that ICK and the thought trap of overgeneralization!)

Whether rejection occurs for reasons like the other person doesn't understand or "click" with your hobbies or lifestyle, or that person doesn't have a natural attraction to you, none of this means you aren't good enough. (I hope this message is getting through!) All it means is that people have preferences! You do, too! Use your newfound confidence to know that you don't have to change who you are to find a relationship; you just need to find the right fit.

There is always someone out there who digs something about you! There are people who like every single type of person on this planet, but you have to like yourself enough to make yourself available and open to the right person! If you start to shut down when things aren't going as you hoped, you might miss the opportunity when something good does come along. Always remember that even if someone has a preference that you don't fit into, it does *not* mean there is something wrong with you! And even if sometimes you get more rejections than you get acceptances, this doesn't have to do with your worth as a person; sometimes it's just a numbers game. And remember that, in the end, all you really need is that one person who you fit well with.

You know that you have the confidence now to hold out for someone who loves and appreciates *all* of you—your physicality, lifestyle, personality, quirks, interests, everything! Don't ever settle for anything less. Understanding how the numbers game works is an important tool for protecting yourself if you face rejection along the way, or if you notice someone else getting more attention than you. But now you know that this has nothing to do with self-worth and that you, too, will find your puzzle piece along the way. Trust!

Differences Are Not Personal

Now we're starting to pull apart the idea that some people may reject you along the way, and we're working on resiliency so that we can handle rejection and protect our soft spot of vulnerability when we bravely show off our True Selves. We're going to review a bit of what we just went over, because some of this stuff can get particularly emotional. I could write a whole book on body image and self-esteem, for both guys and girls, but for this book's purposes, we'll practice this approach of how to be okay with rejection one more time so that rejection (from friends or potential partners, or after a breakup) doesn't shatter all the work you've done on liking yourself. I don't want anything out there to stop you from letting yourself be vulnerable and being your True Self with confidence!

So far in this how-to-be-okay-with-rejection series, we've talked about the superficial (such as lifestyle, hobbies, and physical appearance), because those are a bit easier to understand and to use as examples. But I think you're with me now, and you're following this concept, so we're going to bump it up one more notch. This same concept even applies to your personality. This can be tricky to wrap your emotions around, because people often find personality preferences the most difficult to separate from themselves, which is logical.

People are usually not very emotional about rejection due to lifestyle differences, but they become more emotional when that rejection is about physical attractiveness. They then become most emotional when it comes to rejection regarding personality differences (although physical attractiveness and personality differences can be interchangeable depending on the individuals involved). The reason personality differences are harder to wrap our emotions around is because our personality is usually our soft spot, our True Self, and when it is questioned, it hits right at our core. But the concept is the same as we discussed before around physical preferences and lifestyle differences. Let's look at another example to check out this new variation on the theme.

Let's say a guy doesn't want to date you or be with you because you are "too annoying." First of all, what does that even mean? Maybe that guy really means that you talk too much. Does this mean that you need to curb how much you talk? Now, of course, always self-reflect a bit to see if it is feedback you want to consider, but also keep this in mind: there is someone out there who will think your exuberance is endearing. He will find your energy uplifting, and he won't find this trait annoying at all. He will value this part of you. So, all that this means is that this guy wasn't the right fit for you! Your energy levels didn't work together in a way that made you both happy.

Let's look at another example. What if a guy or girl says you are "too clingy?" Again, self-reflect a bit, but remember, someone out there will instead find this quality reassuring. That

191

person will like that you are always checking in, and will see it as a sign of caring instead of seeing it as needy or controlling. It's all about fit.

For instance, I know lots of couples who seem to do everything together, and for them, it works! They are super happy with that arrangement! But imagine if one person was more independent and the other person wanted the two of them to do everything together—this is where you get people calling each other clingy or avoidant and getting into fights. It doesn't mean either person is wrong, but it does mean that the fit between them isn't right. This is how to keep your confidence up when searching for a relationship that is the right fit for you. By remembering fit and accepting your differences as not personal, you can make it through rejections or breakups that you encounter along the way, keeping your self-esteem and self-confidence intact.

23

How to Be Yourself in a Relationship

Overall Message

Let's sum this idea up. Not only will being your True Self with confidence attract the energy you want, it will allow people to see your energy and connect with you in more meaningful ways, and you won't have to work so hard at pretending all the time. Your body language will open up. You will become more genuine and easier to approach, and people will be attracted to your authenticity. Also, being your True Self when you meet people will then also allow you to be your True Self *during* relationships, which will then be more meaningful and important. Having confidence in your True Self and understanding attraction and rejection as not personal will help you get through the tough stuff in one piece. It will help you understand breakups in a way that doesn't leave you destroyed when things don't go the way you hoped. You will know that rejection is only a matter of fit, not of being "not good enough" as a human. You will know that there is someone out there who will like all the bits about you, numbers game or not, and that just because some people might fit the cultural bell curve of "normal" more or less than you does not in any way mean they are better than you or worse than you. It simply is evidence of statistics at work, and numbers aren't linked to self-worth. You, and everything you are, is where your worth comes from. And you are worthy! And because you know that a deep, meaningful connection is based on relating to someone's True Self, and because you are *so* on your way to being confident and vulnerable and authentic as your True Self, when you do find the right fit, you will be healthy and happy because you won't be pretending and playing games.

You also will have more confidence to say no to relationships that aren't working for you without feeling guilty. You will be able to do what's best for you because you know that if a relationship isn't working out, there is a better fit out there for both of you. That's really as simple as it is—no one is "right" or "wrong" (unless we are talking about abuse, which, again, please tell someone you trust right away), but in relationships, it is all a matter of finding the right fit for your True Self and for the other person's True Self.

Authenticity, vulnerability, and confidence are the true keys to "getting the guy or girl." When the magazines tell you to "do this or do that" differently to "get a guy" or "get a girl," sure, that trick might work, but often only in the short term if it's not your True Self. And now you know that if you have to work so hard to get "that guy" or "that girl," or if you have to play games and pretend, the fit probably isn't a good one for you anyway.

Just as you have to like yourself before you can love yourself, you have to like another person in a relationship before you can love that person. The first steps to move from like to love are being authentic, genuine, and honest—and when you are, the right people will stick around. The ones who leave or the relationships that don't work out weren't the right fit for you. Simple as that!

Now you know that confidence and being vulnerable by being your True Self is the only real "trick" to making relationships work, both with yourself and others. Sometimes you may have to do a bit of searching to find the right fit for you, but if you are true to yourself, if you don't play games, and if you recognize that rejection isn't a measure of your self-worth, you will have solved the mystery of relationships.

I know, I know—that simple advice would put every magazine and blog out of business! But that's why they don't tell you. They can sell more articles if they make you feel like there is some "trick" or some "thing" that you're not doing right or could be doing better! Now you know that it all truly comes down to liking yourself, being confident in yourself, and being vulnerable enough to put yourself out there to attract the right energy, and the right people will come to you.

Wrapping Up

As promised, I worked hard to keep this short and sweet and to the point, and to only give you my best stuff. So it's that time; we're going to wrap things up here. I'd love to know what you think! What would you like to learn more about? What idea would you like me to expand on? Or let me know if you want more exercises or advice on anything that we've touched on so far in this book. I'd love to hear from you! Check out my Facebook page at Cheryl M. Bradshaw, Twitter @CherylMBradshaw, my website and blog at www.cherylmbradshaw.com, and email me at cherylmbradshaw@gmail.com. Feel free to contact me. I will do my best to answer, and to get your great suggestions for what you'd like to see more of in any future books or blog posts. You can also download the app that accompanies this book, PositiveU, to keep working on some of the concepts you have learned throughout.

As we part ways, I want you to know that I'm super proud of you. I know, I know—I sound like a mom, and I don't even really know you! But seriously, I feel like I do know you. To have picked up this book, to have read it with an open mind, and to have hopefully even gotten out a pen and paper a few times and practiced some of these exercises, that takes a special person! Not everyone will have done all of that! It truly shows how dedicated you are to this process, and that shows how much you care. That means you really, truly, are an awesome person. I know I started this book by saying that I knew you were likable, and I can assure you, it is absolutely true. I wish you every ounce of luck in your life, and want only the best for you. I hope you've enjoyed our time together, and I hope you're feeling a little bit more comfortable and happy with your True Self. I hope your ICK has been squished down to size, and I hope you are well on your way to having one of the greatest relationships you will ever experience in life—the one with yourself!

I hope you continue to read and to work on your relationship with yourself and perhaps even move on to books about *loving* yourself! It's always good to learn to like yourself first, but over time, I hope that like turns into love, and that you will be happy to be with yourself no matter where you are in life or how tough things might get. You've got a lot going for you, so keep revisiting that list of positives when you start to question yourself. That list says it all. You're awesome!

Signing off,

Cheryl M. Bradshaw

References

Bearman, P., and J. Moody. 2004. "Suicide and Friendships Among American Adolescents." *American Journal of Public Health* 94, no. 1: 89–95.

Conte, C. 2013. "The Tao of Anger Management: A Yield Theory Approach." Retrieved from Psychotherapy.net: http://www.psychotherapy.net/article/Anger-Management-Conte#section-yield-theory. Accessed September 12, 2013.

Hatzigeorgiadis, A., N. Zourbanos, S. Mpoumpaki, and Y. Theodorakis. 2009. "Mechanisms Underlying the Self-Talk–Performance Relationship: The Effects of Motivational Self-Talk on Self-Confidence and Anxiety." *Psychology of Sport and Exercise* 10, no. 1: 186–92.

Laird, R., B. Bridges, and M. Marsee. 2013. "Secrets from Friends and Parents: Longitudinal Links with Depression and Antisocial Behavior." *Journal of Adolescence* 36, no. 4: 685–93.

Mallinger, A. 2009. "The Myth of Perfection: Perfectionism in the Obsessive Personality." *American Journal of Psychotherapy* 63, no. 2: 103–31.

Padesky, C. 1997. "A More Effective Treatment Focus for Social Phobia?" *International Cognitive Therapy Newsletter* 11, no. 1: 1–3.

Prinstein, M. J. 2007. "Moderators of Peer Contagion: A Longitudinal Examination of Depression Socialization Between Adolescents and Their Best Friends. *Journal of Clinical Child & Adolescent Psychology* 36, no. 1: 159–70.

Cheryl M. Bradshaw is a counselor/therapist at the University of Guelph, and a registered psychotherapist working in private practice. She has previously worked at Sheridan College as a counselor, and has a background in teaching. She has worked with, and continues to support, jack.org, an organization dedicated to youth mental health awareness, empowerment, and leadership in high schools and post-secondary institutions across Canada. Bradshaw resides in Hamilton, ON, Canada, with her husband, Andrew, and their dog, Darwin.

To keep working on some of the concepts you have learned throughout, download the app, PositiveU, a great complement to *How to Like Yourself*.

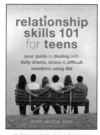